JANE WOOD

ILLUSTRATIONS AND POETRY BY JANE WOOD

TRANSFORMATION THROUGH JOURNAL WRITING

THE ART OF SELF-REFLECTION FOR THE HELPING PROFESSIONS

Jessica Kingsley *Publishers*
London and Philadelphia

First published in 2013
by Jessica Kingsley Publishers
73 Collier Street
London N1 9BE, UK
and
400 Market Street, Suite 400
Philadelphia, PA 19106, USA

www.jkp.com

Library of Congress Cataloging in Publication Data
Wood, Jane, 1954-
  Transformation through journal writing : the art of self-reflection for the helping professions / Jane
Wood.
      p. cm.
  Includes bibliographical references and index.
  ISBN 978-1-84905-347-1 (alk. paper)
  1. Self-perception. 2. Diaries--Authorship. 3. Human services personnel--Psychology. I. Title.
  BF697.5.S43W66 2013
  158.1--dc23

                              2012031193

British Library Cataloguing in Publication Data
A CIP catalogue record for this book is available from the British Library

ISBN 978 1 84905 347 1
eISBN 978 0 85700 690 5

Printed and bound in Great Britain

CONTENTS

ACKNOWLEDGEMENTS

My thanks and gratitude to everyone who has encouraged me in the writing of this book. My loving appreciation to my family for their technical support and proofreading – and to all those who have shared their journals with me.

PREFACE

I have been interested in journal writing ever since I was a moody teenager. In the early years there was the comfort of sharing my life with my silent friend, and exploring my creativity. When I was backpacking around the world, my journal was my record and the consolidation of all my experiences. As a practitioner I keep a reflective journal to investigate, challenge, learn from and congratulate myself.

When I became involved in setting up a distance learning college, I decided that all the students should practise self-reflection; both for self-knowledge and to benefit their future work as practitioners. I asked for a weekly self-reflective journal to be filled in online. The students complied, although it was clear that most of them had never done anything like this before. Some of them disliked it as an invasion of privacy. Many of them were good at telling the story, but found it difficult to learn from their experiences. I persisted with lots of encouragement and some mildly phrased challenges; and I was thrilled to see them making great leaps in self-understanding. It has been my privilege to witness extraordinary self-development over the years with many of the students.

About the same time I began teaching the practitioner–patient relationship to university students. They were asked to keep a clinic log, and were given assignments that demanded self-reflection. Some of them learned quickly, but others were confused about *how* to reflect – or they were resistant to the boundaries set by reflective frameworks. It seemed unlikely that these students would continue with self-reflection after graduation. There are a lot of books on reflective practice available, but I saw the need for one that was addressed directly to the student or practitioner doing the self-reflection. I wanted to encourage them through enthusiasm and example.

When the book was almost complete, I suddenly decided to put everything to the test. I offered weekly feedback in the role of critical friend to practitioners who sent me their journal every week. In our working agreement, I made it clear that I would be using a lot of different techniques to get the practitioners thinking in different ways. The online journal has proved to be one of the most exciting adventures I have undertaken. As if they had nothing to lose, most of the practitioners wrote about the deepest and most disturbing aspects of their work that they had been unable to resolve. Getting them to approach their issues using a variety of techniques was, in many cases, liberating. Again I felt privileged to observe some amazing self-development.

With my confused students in mind, I decided there needed to be journal examples as well as theory in the book. Creating all these journal examples myself has been a fascinating reminder of the value of keeping a journal, whatever form it takes. It has also taken me on a journey from the simplest, most direct form of journal writing through to complex models of self-reflection. Each of my journal examples is an invented scenario, and yet inevitably, as I write them, they come from my inner truth and experience. Inadvertently, I have learned a lot about myself, humbling me and reminding me yet again of the power of self-reflection.

Most, but not all of my journal examples are to do with clinical practice and practice management. Occasionally I stray from this theme, as a gentle reminder that we can reflect on anything that happens in clinic or out of it. We can reflect on experiences, relationships, theory, observations or anything else.

I have chosen the word 'journal' in preference to that of 'diary'. Technically they mean the same thing, but to me journals are more robust and professional, while diaries are perhaps a little more casual and romantic. Also, the word 'journal' comes from the same root as 'journey', a pleasant reminder that the fun and learning are in following the pathway, not reaching the destination. The journeyman is the craftsman who has progressed beyond apprenticeship, but still has not reached mastery. Working with the journal reminds me that I have neither reached the destination nor achieved the mastery. I find this thought gives me freedom and reassurance. If the journal is only a work in progress, it takes away the pressure to be correct or complete, and allows me to take each day as it comes.

It was more difficult to find a suitable word for the person who creates the reflective journal. 'Journalist' has other meanings, as does 'author'. I use the word 'writer' although I am aware that it does not sit comfortably with those engaging with an art journal.

My intention in writing this book is to share both my knowledge about different ways of reflecting and my enthusiasm for reflection as an effective system of self-care and self-development. My hope is that it inspires the reader to experiment with journal writing until they find one or several ways that are both satisfying and effective.

CHAPTER 1

INTRODUCING THE REFLECTIVE JOURNAL

Autumn gold
a child gathers the leaves
into her basket

Self-reflection is a process of observing what happens at work or at home, investigating it in order to understand it, and making suitable changes. It is an ongoing practice of refinement, made up of small steps. It can be done in a group, one to one with a supervisor or critical friend, online with a supervisor, or alone. Doing it with someone else keeps the practitioner focused and on task, and challenges them to understand their issues at a deeper level. Reflecting alone requires more than just mulling it over while travelling home after a hard day at work. It needs dedication, honest inquiry and some way of storing the reflections for future reviews. Working with a self-reflective journal can fulfil all these needs.

Self-reflection encourages deliberate investigation into thoughts, feelings, attitudes, beliefs or intentions, which in turn benefits the practitioner, the patient or client, the whole practice and the profession in general. It suits both traditional practitioners and complementary and alternative medicine (CAM) therapists. Consider the following examples that might come up in practice:

- The boundaries become unclear between practitioner and patient. Which one of them is too demanding and which one too lenient?

- The practitioner always feels incompetent in front of this sort of patient. Where does this originate from?

- The practitioner becomes irritated with what the patient is saying, doing or failing to do. Why does this patient push their buttons?

- The patient fails to turn up for appointments or forgets to pay a private practitioner. Is there a mismatch around expectations?

- The patient doesn't follow the practitioner's recommendations. Has there been a breakdown in communication?

- The patient doesn't get better and this brings up uncomfortable emotions. Why should either the patient or the practitioner feel guilty?

In these cases unreflective practitioners might choose to blame their patients for any discomfort felt within the practitioner–patient relationship, or they might blame themselves for not being the perfect practitioner. Their inner judge or inner justifier might come into the foreground. The inner judge has a critical, parental voice that says, 'You're no good, you messed that one up.' The inner justifier has a self-righteous, childish voice that says, 'It's not my fault, I did the best I could, it was the patient who wasn't cooperating.' But neither of these routes will solve the problem and, life being what it is, these patterns will repeat themselves. In the long run, the practice itself might become dysfunctional or the practitioner might burn out.

A reflective practitioner will make an effort to unpack what has happened on a regular basis in order to make changes for the future, so that it doesn't happen again. Recording this process of exploration and insight in a journal allows each discovery to build upon the previous ones, and consolidates learning. Taylor, writing in *Reflective Practice*, says, 'There is value in reflection as it turns an unconsidered life into one which is consciously aware, self-potentiating and purposeful.' (2000, p.10)

Johari window

An interesting model to help understand the necessity for reflection is the Johari window developed by Luft (1984) and published in *Group Processes: An Introduction to Group Dynamics*. Luft describes four different arenas of awareness of the self. The first two are in the conscious awareness and are known about, while the second two are unconscious.

- *The open arena* is visible to the self and to others. It is the face that is normally shown to the world.

- *The hidden arena* is known to the self but is deliberately kept private from others.

- *The blind arena* can only be seen by others, but not seen by the self. It is through interaction with other people that it is revealed to the self, verbally, non-verbally or through self-reflection.

- *The unknown arena* is completely buried, hidden to all.

We could say that the aim of self-reflection is to open up a proportion of the blind arena and the unknown arena, in order to increase conscious awareness. It is unlikely that anyone would ever have complete access to all their unconscious awareness, and there is probably a limit as to how much this can be done alone without the help of a critical friend or supervisor. That being said, a lot can be revealed through working with a journal.

The wounded healer

What makes someone enter the health professions? It appears to satisfy an inner need to help others and to be liked and appreciated in return. But what lies beneath this? Practitioners who have decided to enter one of the health professions are rarely, if ever, at the peak of their own mental, emotional and physical health. More often they are themselves the wounded healer who seeks (unconsciously) their own inner healing through helping others. If this is so, the practitioner–patient connection will be a symbiotic relationship that feels satisfying when it goes well, but is damaging when it does not.

To understand this further, it is useful to look at the transactional analysis model of ego states. These are inner states of being or experience that involve thinking, feeling and behaving. Simply put, everyone has an inner Parent, Adult and Child formed early on from life experiences and family messages.

The Parent state is unconsciously borrowed from parents or parent figures from the past and can be nurturing or controlling either to the self or to others. The Child state is derived from past thoughts and feelings and can be either natural and free or adapted to strategies for living. The Adult is more balanced, objective and in the present.

Zigmond writes in *Physician Heal Thyself* about 'how doctors take better care of others' needs than their own, and how the nature of their work calls on them to be uncompromisingly "grown-up" in their conduct' (2010, p.5). Zigmond argues that doctors tend to work from Parent and Adult ego states, and suppress their own inner Child while using the patient to fulfil this role. He goes on to say:

> When we deny powerful needs or impulses in ourselves, we will either be intolerant or compulsively solicitous of these attributes in others. If it is the latter, then we can professionalize this problem by working in one of the caring professions. In this area we have licence to seek out and look after the part in other people that we disown or suppress in ourselves. Our needs may then be fulfilled, in an illusory and vicarious way, through a state of mutual dependence. Such an interlocked relationship may be…termed 'symbiotic'. Symbiosis may be thought of as 'benign' when our own needs are peripheral to 'helping the needy'. Conversely, 'malignant' symbiosis is enacted when our own needs become more central, and we are then 'needing the helpless'. (p.5)

Self-reflection helps to address who the healing is for. The value of creating time and space for practitioners to start healing themselves is that patient sessions can be left for patients. This helps to break the rigid dance between practitioner and patient where the practitioner holds Parental power and needs a dependent, Child-like patient. They can both begin to work together on an Adult–Adult level.

The need to rescue others

Another useful model is the drama triangle, first introduced by Karpman (1968). There are three roles, those of Victim, Persecutor and Rescuer, which can arise within any interaction between two or three people. These are like subconscious role-plays, and have no relationship to genuine cases of hardship. Anyone can take any role, and there can be several changes of role within a short space of time.

There is often a favourite or default role that each person slips into the most easily.

Victims appear to be helpless, complaining and dependent. They act as if they are powerless, and wait for others to do the problem solving. They can feel that life isn't fair and appeal for help, but they aren't good at taking advice. Persecutors feel they are superior and maintain this position by belittling or controlling others. They can be angry and aggressive and enjoy conflict. They can have fixed ideas about right and wrong and are quite selfish. Rescuers also have a feeling of superiority, which they use to help others while at the same time keeping them powerless. They can be patient, understanding, responsible, placating and avoiding of conflict. They can put others first and find it difficult to maintain boundaries or say 'No'.

Many patients go into the Victim stance, feeling persecuted by their illness, or whoever they perceive has caused the illness, or the previous practitioner who failed to cure them. Many practitioners find themselves responding by going into the Rescuer role. Some are compulsive Rescuers, especially those who have had a history of being the Rescuer since childhood – for example, children who have had to care for their parents emotionally or physically. This tendency to go into the Rescuer role has its own satisfaction at first, making them feel good at having helped someone. They like the appreciation they get in return. But in the long run it is not healthy, because practitioners become dependent on having patients in order to rescue them and feel good. They can lose boundaries, giving patients extra time, extra care, special discounts and so on. Eventually this becomes burdensome and can weaken the practitioner's health or self-confidence. It also prevents patients from taking responsibility for their own health and self-healing. If patients do not get better, practitioners might go into Persecutor mode or arrive at the supervision session in Victim mode.

Practitioners who are aware of this tendency and reflect regularly on their interactions with patients or clients can form much healthier relationships. Through observing themselves, they can notice whether they have a balanced relationship with their patients, or whether they have an emotional response. They can notice when they are allowing boundaries to be pushed or dissolved, and they can start to examine what this means.

Commitment to continuing professional development

Nowadays, it is not enough for practitioners and therapists to achieve their initial qualification. There is an expectation that they will engage with continuing professional development (CPD), and this is written into many different codes of ethics. For example, The Society of Homeopaths 'Code of Ethics and Practice' (2010) says, 'Registered and student clinical members should regularly monitor and evaluate their clinical skills and actively extend their knowledge base and their own personal development through continuing professional development' (p.6).

CPD takes many forms, including attending conferences, seminars, further training courses and studying at home with new publications. Self-reflection is an important aspect of CPD, because it is a way of looking at the practice in order to improve it for the future.

The benefits for practitioner, patient and practice

At its most basic level, the journal can be used as a record or memorandum of what needs to be discussed with a supervisor or team. But beyond that, it can provide a safe space for self-supervision. Working continuously with people who are unwell in body or mind takes its toll on the practitioner or therapist. The work is often stressful and sometimes traumatic. In an ideal world, all practitioners would have the opportunity to work with a supervisor in order to reflect on, and learn from, their clinical experiences. In some professions supervision is mandatory, but in others it is voluntary or simply not available for financial, location, timetabling or historical reasons. Practitioners who struggle on without help run the risk of becoming dysfunctional in practice or burning out. The solution is either to work with a critical friend such as a colleague, or enter into self-supervision using the reflective journal.

Self-reflection in a working journal deliberately creates a little space or distance between practitioners and their issues, which over time helps to build up objectivity. The journal is a physical, concrete place that is outside the busy, multi-tasking mind. It formalises reflection and adds detachment, making it easier for practitioners to engage with their own understanding without being controlled by the need to self-justify or judge themselves.

Practitioners gain a lot through keeping a journal. Exploring their own attitudes, beliefs and values can lead to a reassessment of their motivations creating a much healthier attitude in their work. Exploring their role with a patient, such as through a basic transactional analysis model, can reveal complex patterns that can be exchanged for clearer, more adult interactions. Writing about patient trauma can help to discharge it so that practitioners don't go on holding the trauma after the patient has left.

If the reflective journal is used regularly, with flexibility, honesty and depth of inquiry, it can provide both support and self-care for the practitioner. Adams, writing in *Journal to the Self*, says: '*Get it out of your system!* Your journal is a perfectly appropriate place to express yourself – *all* of yourself. Tell the complete truth faster. Fifteen minutes of ventilating on paper can save you a migraine headache' (1990, p.39; emphasis in original).

Patients benefit as well. Through questioning their interview skills and assessing their strengths and weaknesses in the consultation, practitioners will improve their technique. Their clinical observation skills through all the senses will develop as they write about cases or make patient descriptions. With complex cases, the practitioners can clarify their thoughts and decide on possible treatment plans.

The exciting opportunity

Journals can provide a safe place for reacting honestly to the present, exploring the past in order to understand it, and preparing for the future. They can offer a quiet time outside the busyness of daily life in which the writer can begin to understand their true self. They offer self-care for the practitioner or therapist. They provide a learning opportunity where everything is fed back into the practice, benefiting both the practitioner and future patients. They hold the exciting opportunity for transformation into a more confident, more effective and more clear-sighted self.

CHAPTER 2

GETTING STARTED

Empty screen
the cat waits for me to start
with wide eyes

All journals begin with an empty book or a blank screen. There is a quiet moment, a pause of pleasurable anticipation or hesitation before the adventure of journal writing begins. It is difficult to foresee what it will become. Will it be an occasional outlet, a robust support, a demanding chore or a working tool for self-therapy?

For most people, the reflective journal is a personal concern, never to be made public. It is an ongoing project, carefully built up with regular entries but without a foreseeable conclusion. A journal is as individual as its writer and can be serious, purposeful, therapeutic, creative, spiritual or anything else. It can be initiated with a clear intention or a vague hope it will be helpful; and as the journal progresses it forms its own character.

Some journals have a strong intellectual purpose. For example, they can be a personal record of the writer's work experience with a cool, objective analysis about what has been learned. They might be a work in progress for intense thinking and intellectual growth, with discussions of theory and ongoing development of ideas. They can be an evaluation of projects that have been undertaken or topics studied as a necessary part of CPD.

In contrast, other journals are far more emotional. These can provide a safe space for emotional outpourings, allowing the writer to discharge strong feelings and subsequently face the world from a clearer perspective. They can be the undisturbed venue for emotional understanding and self-therapy, benefiting both the writer and those they come into contact with. They can be a silent confessional for secret hopes, wishes or fears, subjects that the writer does not want to express in front of other people.

Journals can be a place of calm peacefulness where the writer's spirituality can be experienced. They can contain prayers, blessings or conversations with God. For some people the power of prayer is increased by writing it down. The journal can be the place where the day's events are hastily thrown down in order to clear the mind before meditating. The creative act of connecting with the journal can provide peaceful downtime.

The journal itself can fulfil many roles. It can be a silent friend, a compassionate therapist, a nurturing parent, a wise supervisor or a keeper of secrets. A journal can act as the best of friends, quietly supportive and good-natured, listening to everything with no judgement and demanding nothing from the writer. In the role of therapist, the journal provides the safe space of the clinic, with compassionate listening and encouragement for the writer to think for themselves and find their own solutions to problems. As a nurturing parent, the journal provides comfort and reassurance, allowing a temporary regression into immaturity, so the writer can emerge refreshed and stronger. As a wise supervisor, the journal encourages the writer to challenge themselves and develop professionally.

There is a tremendous freedom in creating a personal journal, because there are no rules or boundaries about content or style. Rainer (1978) writing in *The New Diary*, celebrates 'the untamed freedom of the diary' (she uses the words 'diary' and 'journal' interchangeably).

> The diary is the only form of writing that encourages total freedom of expression. Because of its very private nature, it has remained immune to any formal rules of content, structure or style. As a result the diary can come closest to reproducing how people really think and how consciousness evolves. (p.11)

The only drawback is when the journal writer does not know the options available or cannot see the way to make the most of them. Few journals are accessible for public reading and those that are, have probably been edited. It is ironic that the freedom of writing a personal journal can be talked about but is seldom seen. The newcomer to journal writing can very rarely have a role model.

It is worth taking the time to think about what you want from your reflective journal and reviewing this from time to time (see Figure 2.1).

Figure 2.1 What do you want from your journal?

Finding a journal style that suits you

The structure of the brain is in two hemispheres, and each side is responsible for different functions. In general, most people have a dominant side to their brain that affects how they receive and process information. The left brain deals with rational thought, logic, linear, analytic and sequential thinking, calculating and mathematics. Left-brained people tend to look at the details, and put them together to make a whole. The right side of the brain processes emotion, feeling, intuition, creativity and emotional connections within a group. Right-brained people prefer to look at the bigger picture first and then look at the details.

Western thinking tends to prioritise the left brain, which is rational and logical. Accuracy and analysis are perceived to be more dependable than intuitive leaps, but for those people who are right brained, creativity and intuition provide the deepest learning.

Self-reflection using a working journal can be done from either side of the brain or it can integrate both. A mainly left-brained, rational writer will be attracted to a structured journal, with events recorded in sequence. They will be interested in accuracy, and might want to work from a reflective model or framework. A mainly right-brained, creative writer will explore the visual presentation on the page, and might work with drawings, colour or poetry.

Every writer is individual and many gravitate towards their preferred style – either more rational or more intuitive. But Western-style education teaches a left-brained, formal writing style, and sometimes this is so ingrained that a journal writer can automatically choose this style above their natural preference. This will probably make journal writing a chore and in some cases there can be so much resistance they simply give up. Giving themselves permission to work creatively might make all the difference.

There are strong arguments that self-reflection is equally effective when it is non-verbal or holds the minimum of words. Charts, diagrams, drawings, mind maps and 'cut and paste' are all valid methods of self-reflection, allowing the practitioner to explore intuitively.

I suggest there is a lot to be learned from trying out new journal styles or different methodologies. It takes you away from the familiar pathways of thinking and feeling and can open up many blind spots. You might find you actually prefer ways of working that you hadn't considered previously, or that different ways of working suit different issues. The more you can experiment with different journal styles, the more you will increase your options and develop self-learning.

What will the journal look like?

Journals can be created publicly or privately, on paper or on the computer. A handwritten journal can be written in a finely bound book bought for the purpose – or on scraps of paper. Some people like to have a friendly book of the size, shape, appearance and paper quality that appeals to them visually and tactilely. For those writing in notebooks or on scraps of paper, there can be a box file for storage, or the entries can be fastened into a clip file. Computer journals can be held in a document folder or printed and filed into a ring binder.

The way in which different people write is completely individual, according to the mood and purpose of the writer. The journal can be left brained, serious, quiet and dedicated. It can be right brained, flamboyant, expanding all over the page, with drawings, crossings out and changes in the topic. Journal entries can be routine or irregular. Rainer writes in *The New Diary*, 'Allow yourself to write whenever you feel like it, when you need the emotional release, when you need to clarify your thoughts, or when the spirit moves you.' (1978, p.35) Topics can be anything at all with nothing that is off-limits. Entries can range from minimal five-minute notes and abbreviated bullet points to lengthy discussions and rambling descriptions of feelings.

Some journals need to be well written, because they will be shared with a critical friend, supervisor or tutor. But the journal that is written for the self can be like the spoken word, stretching all possibilities of structure, grammar and spelling, constantly in a state of creation. The rules of the written word don't need to apply here. Thinking doesn't need to be linear, spelling doesn't need to be accurate and sentences don't need to be coherent. Old memories of school essays can be set aside. Adams (1990), writing in *Journal to the Self*, says:

> You'll find that your journal doesn't care if you spell words correctly, put commas in the proper place, or scribble in the margins. You can draw a picture, write in circles around the page, write big and sloppy or tiny and precise. Journal writing is a near-perfect hobby: inexpensive, always available, no special equipment or skills required, expandable or contractible to fit any time allotment. (p.14)

Public or private?

Some journals are intended to be made public – for example, when reflective journals are part of professional training or a university degree. They can be a mandatory part of the course to ensure that the students practise the skills of critical thinking or self-reflection. The journal may be checked by the tutor who might give feedback, which necessitates a more formal style of writing. Other forms of public journal are when a practitioner chooses to write a blog or a self-reflective article that will be published in a newsletter.

However, most reflective journals are kept private. They are written for self-development and professional development. Like the pearl in the oyster, they are built up layer after layer over time. In rereading the journal, further pearls might be discovered.

Keeping the journal private

Even the most minimal journal reveals something about the inner life of the writer, and the fuller and more detailed it becomes, the more it could potentially expose. It is often too personal to be on public view because the character of the writer becomes embedded into both the writing style and the content. Keeping the journal private is in many cases a realistic measure, although the very act of secrecy can make it more interesting to others.

There are many practical reasons for keeping a journal hidden. It might contain strong emotions or controversial opinions, which at the time of writing were a therapeutic outpouring of feeling, to be rationalised and understood at a later date. It might contain hopes, wishes and fears that are not for public viewing. The journal writer might be temporarily disloyal to colleagues, friends or family, or they might mix up reality with visualisation. They might have chosen a relaxed style that is ungrammatical, misspelled or full of vocabulary that would be cleaned up before showing it to anyone else. Altogether, many journals contain controversial material that could cause criticism, embarrassment or pain should anyone else read it. Even if the ultimate intention is to share the journal, or publish it, it should only be read when the journal writer declares it fit to read.

It is best to create clear boundaries around the journal. Rainer (1978), writing in *The New Diary*, says that it is the responsibility of the journal writer to keep the journal private.

> It's unfair to present those you care about with the temptation of the diary left out in the open and expect them to resist their curiosity on the basis of good manners. The diary has its own body language which may belie its owner's stated wishes. If it is accessible, it seems to say, 'Read me!' (p.48)

In contrast, some long-term journal writers report that they care less and less about would-be readers. It could be that the fear of exposure attracts more people to look at it, and a casual attitude with few or no boundaries makes it less attractive.

Here are some suggestions about how to create good boundaries around a journal.

Name the first page: The first page can have a short paragraph expressing ownership and privacy, such as 'These are my personal thoughts and not for public viewing. Please obtain my permission if you want to read it and do not be disappointed if I refuse.'

Put your photo on the first page: A serious photo of yourself inside the first page creates eye contact with anyone who opens your journal. Put a message with it that makes it explicit that they should not read any further. For example, 'Stop! Don't go any further. This is my personal journal and it is not for public viewing.'

Hide the journal: Choose a safe or unexpected place to keep your journal.

Tell other people explicitly: You can tell other people at work or at home that you are writing a journal and that it is private. They are asked to respect this privacy.

Differentiating the various types of journals

Some journals are written with a specific aim in view, while others develop and evolve over time. There are no perfect formulas and no model answers. Every journal is as individual as its writer, so it is impossible to classify different journals into genres or types. Yet for the ease of writing and the subsequent reading of this book, I have gathered them into categories and labelled them. I am aware that these are temporary groupings at best, and that all journals will easily break out of my imposed boundaries. My hope is that discussing some of the options available will stimulate the reader's enthusiasm to try something different.

The narrative journal: The narrative journal contains a record of personal thoughts, emotions, observations or events that happen at work, in clinic or with clients. This journal starts as a record and only becomes reflective with the use of self-questioning and dialogue with the narrative (Chapter 3).

The learning journal: This focuses on a programme of study, with reflective observations and discussions about what has been learned, leading to further research. It can be used throughout a long training period or as a place to gather material, ideas and thoughts for an assignment. This journal will probably come to an end when the topic of study is completed (Chapter 3).

The self-reflective or working journal: Self-reflection is the regular, deliberate examination of issues as they arise, as a way of increasing self-knowledge. This feeds into self-development, with further benefits to clients and the profession. A whole range of different styles and methodologies can be used (Chapters 4 and 5).

The positive achievement journal: A positive achievement is anything initiated by the writer that makes them feel good. Listing positive achievements every day boosts self-confidence (Chapter 4).

The art or creative journal: Using creative tools provides a different form of self-reflection whereby the writer feels (rather than thinks) their way to a conclusion. Activities include drawing, painting, poetry, photography, singing, mime, montage, scrapbooking and playing with toys. The journal needs a brief summary in writing as a record of the creative process and reflective insights (Chapter 6).

The scrapbook journal or single page montage: This is often a colourful, vibrant mixture of journal writing, artwork, pictures and memorabilia. It frequently has a relaxed style, often deliberately mixing together the formal and informal in a fun and cheerful presentation. It can be used for a specific task or project, such as a learning journal (Chapter 6).

Reflective frameworks and models: Working within a specific model or using a reflective framework provides structure for self-reflection. Such methods are useful for issues that need to be thought through carefully in order to make changes to tasks, productivity, relationships or outcomes. Frameworks ensure that reflection is done logically and conscientiously (Chapter 7).

Visualisation: There are three main forms of visualisation that can be used as part of self-reflection. Creative visualisation can loosely be termed a goal-setting tool that uses the power of the imagination. Exploratory visualisation is a method suitable for opening up blind spots. Maintenance visualisation helps with clearing out brain clutter and negative thinking (Chapter 8).

Reflective worksheets: Reflective worksheets demand deep self-reflection. They contain a minimum of questions that encourage the writer to think deeply and give considered answers. They are similar to the reflective framework, but usually work on the emotions rather than a specific incident (Chapter 9).

The dream journal: This is a record of a writer's dreams, written down as an exploration into the subconscious. At first the dreams are difficult to remember, but it gets easier if there is a strong intention to remember them and a morning routine of writing them down first thing (not written about further in this book).

A few recommendations

There are no rules and regulations about how to write a journal and every journal is as individual as its writer. However, I do have some recommendations that will enable the novice journal writer to get the most from their journal.

Choose an attractive format: Choose a notebook or format for writing or creative work that feels good for you; and decide where you will keep it.

Use it often: Get in the habit of writing or creating regularly, even if it is brief. Like any muscle that hasn't been exercised for a while, you may be a little bit stiff at first. Make journal entries a part of your routine, such as every morning, after each session with a client, after each staff meeting, or every time you have an evening free.

Work with freedom: Everything you choose to work with is okay, so don't impose rules on yourself and don't be shy. Follow your intuition and choose whatever style of writing, creating or developing your journal that suits you. Give yourself permission to have fun, play and frankly express your moods in their full rainbow colours. Try out new ways of journaling to stretch yourself.

Dare to go: Have the courage to explore parts of your inner self that you haven't examined before. Work with depth, honesty and openness.

Watch out for your inner judge: Your inner judge always wants to criticise you and put you down. To counteract it, remember to congratulate yourself on what goes well. Note down past and present achievements to cheer yourself up on low days.

Watch out for your inner justifier: Your inner justifier always wants you to be in the right. It cannot find fault with you and prefers to blame the other person. But you will learn far more about yourself if you admit you might have been wrong, and explore why – in the privacy of your journal.

Keep what you write or create. Even the most important discoveries about yourself can easily be forgotten, and bland entries that seem to be lacking any depth or insight may contain seeds that germinate later.

Date every entry. Dating each entry really helps when you are rereading your journal. You will be able to see your progress in some areas, and your stuckness in others. You will see patterns of intense journaling every day, and silences when you were too busy to write or create.

Have fun. Include things that make you laugh and lift your spirits.

Be kind to yourself. The journal is a valuable tool for self-care. Through consciously accepting your strengths and working on your weaknesses, you can nurture yourself.

Facing the empty page

For some people, starting a journal feels like a pleasurable indulgence. You might have a history of childhood or teenage diaries, or you are already writing an online blog, or you correspond regularly with loved ones abroad or you are generally attracted to creative forms of expression.

Other people find the thought of keeping a journal quite daunting. You might have had no occasion to write for many years. Like adult students returning to further education and having to write essays, you might feel overwhelmed by the task. You might have difficulties with writing because of childhood experiences, such as being told off for writing in a way that didn't fit in with the perceived notion of correct grammar, spelling and handwriting. You might feel self-conscious doing self-reflection, or you might not be giving yourself enough time to sit down and think. You might compensate by telling yourself that you have no issues that need exploring further.

If you have a strong inner resistance, you might find you forget to write your journal for weeks at a time, or you lose the journal, or you don't have enough time to write. The reasons for resistance are many and worth exploring. Resistance can arise from a simple mismatch between your own learning style and your vision of how the journal should be written. For example, if you naturally gravitate towards an experiential or creative way of learning, you will feel constrained, restless, miserable or frustrated with formal writing. Finding a new methodology can be liberating.

If you feel resistant, it might help to change your thinking about the journal. If you can see it literally or symbolically as the dog-eared notebook that is your friend and companion, it can be less threatening. Remember it is a tool written by you, for your own benefit. It can take any shape or form that suits you. Try out different methodologies, and follow any system or style, according to your mood or what you want to write about.

Your journal should come with permission to play. The value of having fun is enormous. It provides relief from any task-based objective, it develops your sense of humour as well as your imagination, and it enables spiritual expansion. Play is how children learn, consolidating experiences, rehearsing for the future, extending the imagination and making sense of their world and their relationships. The aim of reflective practice is to make sense of your world and your relationships, to consolidate your experiences, to rehearse for the future and above all to learn.

I recommend that you begin with small journal entries but write them frequently and put your inner judge on hold. Explore lots of different techniques, and indiscriminately congratulate yourself on whatever you produce, simply because you have taken the time to do something. The following reflective exercises might be useful. As with the rest of this book, feel free to change or extend the exercises in any way. They are only suggestions, not instructions.

Discover your learning style

Everyone is different when it comes to learning styles. Some people are very flexible and can work within a wide range. Others find some ways of working really suit them while they cannot get on with other methods. Yet others have only one style that really works for them.

Don't take your learning style for granted. Your most comfortable style might have been overridden by the needs of your educational system. You might find that, if there was a high pupil–teacher ratio, the teacher probably chose left-brained, logical and intellectual teaching methods in order to control the class. Experiencing, investigating or discussing take more time and are better facilitated in small groups, but maybe you had no opportunity to try these out.

Finding the facts: This is the person who likes to do independent research. They read books, check the internet, take notes and ask questions. They may like to relate self-reflection to theory.

Thinking about it: This person thinks carefully and analyses the information. Sometimes they can be slow but they are thorough and good at critical thinking. They might prefer a reflective framework or model to work from, so they can work step by step.

Experiencing it: This type of person needs to take part in an experience to learn. They can reflect very well if they can relate learning to an experience. They may prefer to work with a critical friend or supervisor or, when working alone, they might prefer a reflective task that includes some activity. However, they sometimes need to push themselves to write up notes after doing experiential reflection.

Visual learning: The visual learner likes to see it to understand it. They might be artistic and want to do drawings, or they might prefer to work with mind maps and charts. They like visualisations. If they are writing, they want it to look good on the page.

Aural learning: The aural student learns through listening. They like to listen to lectures or recorded information, or have music on while they are studying or reflecting.

Tactile learning: This person learns through touching. Even when they were a child at school, they played with their pencil while they were listening to the teacher. They like practical activities and reflective tasks.

Talking it through: This learner needs to say things with their own voice to learn something. They like to work with a critical friend or supervisor and, if alone, they might say the words out loud while they are writing.

Here is a short exercise that will help you identify your preferred learning style.

Exercise 1

Think back to when you were at junior school. What can you remember learning and what did you enjoy learning?

Then think about when you were in high school or in further education (college or university). What can you remember about how you went about learning, and how effective it was?

Finally, think about learning a practical skill, such as playing a musical instrument or driving a car. How easy or difficult was this for you?

Using the senses

Working with the senses encourages you to tune into your physical body, grounding you in what you know or have observed of reality.

This exercise should be started with a short meditation or quiet time. Sit in a chair with both feet on the floor or sit cross-legged on the floor and your eyes either closed or looking at something neutral. The aim is to gently relax your body, which in turn can slow down or quieten the thinking mind. This process creates a deliberate space or time gap between your busy thoughts, which enables the creative process.

While you sit quietly, start to breathe deeper into your lungs, making the out-breath slightly longer than the in-breath. When your breathing has settled into a slow, steady pattern, allow each out-breath to relax you further, loosening all the little muscles around your face and neck. Take one deeper inhalation and let it out as a sigh. Let your body relax and allow your weight to be taken and held by the chair or the ground.

When you feel ready, you can start to work with your five senses. You can begin with whichever one you prefer, but probably the sense of hearing will be the easiest. Focus on what you can hear, such as the sound of your own breathing, the sounds drifting in from outside, like traffic noise or birdsong, or the sound of other people in the same building. Don't try to analyse or work with these sounds in any way. Just be aware of them. Then imagine for a few moments some very loud sounds, such as the refuse collection lorry, or an aeroplane taking off. If you choose to go to an extreme sound, such as a rock concert, remember the feeling of the sound vibrating throughout your entire body.

Now move on to another of the five senses. You might choose to work with vision next, but keep your eyes closed. You can imagine seeing something very simple, such as a candle flame or an apple, and then something very complicated with colour or pattern, such as the leaves on a tree on a windy day, a patterned piece of fabric or a shelf of books in the library.

When you work with your sense of smell, try to imagine three or four different odours, such as lemon, garlic, pepper, curry, perfume, flowers or wild-growing herbs. As you call each smell to mind, stay with it briefly before you move on to the next one. When you think about taste, take your time to imagine sitting down at a meal and experiencing different tastes. You might choose to include the four different polarities of sweet, sour, bitter and salty, or you might choose more complex tastes.

When you visualise your sense of touch, again it is stimulating to work with contrast. You can imagine stroking something soft, like velvet or your cat's fur, and then imagine something that is harsh to touch, such as running your fingertips along the wiry side of Velcro® or a rough concrete wall.

When you finish this visualisation, come gently back to the present and, when you are ready, try one or more of the following exercises.

Exercise 1
Make notes in your journal of all the different sensual experiences that you imagined. Then consider what memories they evoked, and whether these were pleasurable or not.

Exercise 2
Take a large sheet of paper and, working fast, make a quick, instinctive, impressionistic image of the different senses that you were visualising. Have fun translating the multidimensional senses into a two-dimensional image on paper, using colour, texture, line and energy. After you have finished, notice how you felt during the creative process and write a few notes as a memo.

Exercise 3

Take your camera around your house, office or garden, and take photos to represent each of the senses. Be as creative as you want, and break any rules that are lurking in the back of your mind about what you ought to do. After you have finished, write a simple list in bullet points about how you felt during the visualisation and during the photography. Notice if these were the same or different.

Exercise 4

Walking around your house, office or garden, engage with your senses and experience colour, sound, smell, touch and taste. Then make some notes on how these felt compared with your visualisation.

Exercise 5

Write a short story about an everyday activity, such as having a bath or shower, preparing a meal or doing some exercise. Include all the senses in your writing.

JOURNAL EXAMPLE

It was late afternoon when I went out for my walk today, and when I got to the park the sun was low on the horizon, casting long shadows from the trees and the people walking. There were gentle breezes at ground level, but there must have been a brisk wind high up because the clouds were dancing across the sky, grey, white and cream with vivid bursts of blue. A brown, feathery dog came rushing up towards me, barking with excitement and waving its flag-like tail, but suddenly stopped in embarrassment when it realised it had mistaken me for someone else. The sun was in its eyes.

The wind had loosened some pinecones, and I stooped to pick one up from the grass. It felt harsh and prickly in my hand and an awkward shape to hold easily. One side was sticky with resin, which left a black smear on my fingers. I put it up to my nose and inhaled deeply, picking up the smell of pine and a slightly animal smell, dusty and feral. I put it down quickly.

I was very pleased to be walking well. The weakness in my knee seems to be a thing of the past, an old injury to be forgotten. The ever-changing beauty of the sky, and the delightful feeling of walking briskly, suddenly filled me with a rush of happiness, and I felt I wanted to smile at everyone I met.

Ahead of me on the path, a young mother had picked up her toddler and was trying to put her into a pushchair, but the little girl had gone rigid with indignation and wouldn't sit down. She began to scream loudly, kicking her mother and twisting her body. I admired the mother's patience and dexterity, and smiled at her as I drew near. The child paused in her screams, and I said quietly, 'You've got some resistance there.'

The mother glanced up, saying, 'It's time to go home; we've had enough of walking in the park.'

The child suddenly collapsed inwards, and snuggled up to her mother, the picture of a shy and complacent toddler. Feeling amused, I decided to collude with the mother, saying, 'I expect she is tired, and would like a ride in the pushchair to get home.'

The little girl shot me a suspicious look from underneath her curly fringe, and then said to her mother, 'pushchair'. The mother smiled broadly at me and neatly settled the child into the seat and fastened the seatbelt. I continued on my walk.

JOURNAL EXAMPLE

REFLECTIONS

I did the meditation and visualisation of all the senses, and then did a painting of them (see Figure 2.2). Most of the colours are bright, with green, yellow and the rich carroty colour of the broth but the onion is dull brown. The sounds are the gentle plup-plup of the broth, and the harsh sound of the carrots being grated. The smells are sharp, pungent onion and sweet, aromatic thyme. The tastes are the simple acidic lemon and complex broth. The touch is of the harsh grater and the hot pan.

I've got some interesting contrasts here! The visual sense and the tastes were the most important to me. I was the least concerned about the touch, and I've realised I didn't include a soft-touch item here at all. Even the thyme is quite twiggy.

Figure 2.2 Painting used to visualise all the senses

Boosting your memory

Many modern Western societies have lost the art of memorising. Our ancestors were much better at it, especially at times when writing materials were not very accessible. Recording conversations in the journal is a great way of training the memory. It is also a useful record showing the ebb and flow of ideas between two or more people. You might find that you remember your own remarks more clearly than those of the other person, but this doesn't matter. You are doing it for your own benefit and even if it is lopsided there is still a lot you can learn from it.

Exercise 1

Begin with stretching your memory by recalling snippets of conversations. You can do this while you are involved in mindless physical activities such as walking, travelling to work or doing chores around the house. This will open up more interest in recollecting speech, and from there you can start writing short pieces of dialogue in your journal. At first this can feel like trying to remember your dreams, but gradually you will become more and more efficient at it.

Exercise 2

The next time you're watching a movie, tell yourself you will be tested on it the following day, and make an effort to memorise certain key features, such as the names of three or four of the main actors, the plot, one particular scene and a few sentences of dialogue. The next day, write down as much as you remember in your journal. Notice any patterns about what you have remembered and what you have forgotten.

Exercise 3

Working with a good friend, colleague or relative, invite them out for coffee and take a notepad and pen with you. Ask them if they mind you taking brief notes as you chat. Explain that you are working on improving your memory. As you talk together, write down the key words of the conversation, but do not attempt to write whole sentences. Later try to write up the conversation using the key words in your notebook to jog your memory.

JOURNAL EXAMPLE

I had lunch with Tim – pasta and salad – and got into a very interesting and intense discussion about an article he had been reading. A couple of weeks ago we were fascinated by an online article describing how Asian parents pressurise their children into studying and learning, with the assumption that when they have mastered it they will get enjoyment; while Western parents encourage their children to enjoy studying, but they achieve less on the whole because children are naturally lazy.

This morning Tim had been reading a counterargument, that suggested that Asians could grow up lacking essential communication skills, and sometimes had to be retrained later in life in how to make friends. The article suggested that some American Asian males didn't know how to talk to women because they had been too busy studying to form relationships during their college and university years.

Of course these are all generalisations, but I was fascinated by the idea. 'So that would mean that Westerners are putting more effort into social skills when they are children and teenagers, while Asians are learning how to study effectively, and get good jobs?'

Tim thought about that for a moment and then laughed, 'I agree that sometimes Western teenagers put a higher priority on social skills and dating, rather than studying. But if they all go to a mixed-race school, you would've thought the Asians would learn social skills – but apparently not.'

'But don't you see,' I replied, 'it represents the two halves of the brain! The Asians are putting all their emphasis on left-brained, logical thinking, while the Westerners are interested in relationships and the bigger picture. Both are important but it will depend upon what sort of job you want. If Asians have been put through brain-training, they will be ideal for money-earning jobs that require mathematical thinking and analysis. If Westerners have spent their youth developing social skills, they will be ideal for jobs that require communication.'

Tim was not so happy with this, being a mathematician himself. 'Hey, you can be a mathematician and still make friends!'

'Well, you can say that, because you're a Westerner and you weren't pressurised by your parents to study every day of the week! But what interests me are the cultural assumptions, assuming this is correct. This suggests that Asians put more emphasis on hard work and achievement...'

Tim interrupted me, 'But we knew that anyway. Just look at the Asians who were in our secondary school, and compare the grades they got with those of the other kids.'

'Yes, but what this latest article suggests is that they pay a price, by missing out on social interaction, because it is put at a much lower priority.'

CHAPTER 3

NARRATIVE JOURNALS

Delicate pearls
adorn the spider's web
early morning

The narrative journal is fresh, genuine, uncomplicated and often the writer's first venture into journal keeping. It contains descriptions of people, events or day-to-day life. It is often written from the heart but it is not necessarily a logical commentary. In it factual records can blend easily with emotional outpourings while thoughts can flow in any direction.

At its simplest, the narrative journal can be a descriptive, historical record. Writing it provides some quiet time in which to download thoughts and emotions onto paper or screen. Inside the mind, thoughts are not linear but interconnecting with other thoughts, jumping topics and forever in motion. Expressing them in the journal creates a space between the thinker and the thoughts, allowing time to slow down and for the mind to calm down. In the same way, if the journal is used as an outlet for the emotions, it can slow down or bring to a halt the constant replaying of passionate, emotive and destructive thoughts, thereby reducing stress.

However, the descriptive, historical record is not reflective and doesn't become so until the writer chooses to re-engage with the subject matter in a more objective way. Once the writer begins to challenge what they have written or view it from a different angle, they open up the possibility of learning from it.

The narrative journal is never a completely accurate or factual record. Everyone makes observations through the lens of their own interests, knowledge and experience. When several people are observing the same client or the same occurrence, they will notice different things and tell a different version of it. Besides this, within most experiences there will be aspects that could not be fully understood or directly observed. Most people will want to fill in the gaps in order to make sense of their experience. They will make an intelligent guess and choose likely explanations. In doing so, they construct a story out of the experience, guessing at what they don't know and maybe even embroidering it to make it more meaningful. There is nothing wrong with this, but anyone interested in self-reflection should be aware that stories written as a narrative journal entry are open to challenge.

A journal provides the opportunity to dialogue with a story. If the story is just written out as a statement, there it will remain. Worse than that, writing it in the journal can sometimes set it in stone, together with all its little inaccuracies. If practitioners are using a journal for the purposes of self-reflection, there needs to be some self-questioning. They can explore either the content of the writing (what happened) or the style (how it was presented). Working with the content allows them to review what happened, evaluate and analyse it. An example of this is the reflective framework (see Chapter 7).

Working with the style of writing is a different way of reflecting and equally rewarding. This method accepts that there is a choice in how a piece of written work is presented, and then examines that choice. Reflective questions can be asked, such as why the piece of work was presented in this way at this time.

One way of doing this is to describe the issue spontaneously, allowing the process of filling in the gaps to take place. Afterwards, the writer can start to question why they wanted to push a story in a certain direction, rewriting or exaggerating some features, or forgetting to write about others. They can identify where they filled in the gaps. This can reveal further information about the self. It needs a level of objectivity and might be easier to do with a critical friend. If it is being done alone, it can be useful to ask such questions as:

- Which parts of the story do I know to be absolutely true, and which might I have changed a little bit?

- Where have I filled in the gaps?

- Who was I writing this for? Who is my imaginary audience?

- Is there a part of me (for example, my inner Parent or Child) who would benefit from this type of story?

- What does it accomplish?

- What bits of the experience did I deliberately leave out, and why?

- What did I gain from leaving them out?

- What bits of the experience did I embellish and if so why?

Another way of working with the writing style comes after accepting that it is natural to turn experience into an interesting story to make sense of it – and to do it deliberately. Examples of this would be to grossly exaggerate some aspects, create an alternative ending or turn the story into poetry or a play. The imaginative aspects of the written text can be put in a different colour or font, and can be followed by further reflection.

Transformation through narrative

The habit of reflecting on thoughts, emotions, observations or experiences provides numerous and cumulative benefits. When you make a commitment to writing a journal, you have contracted to having regular, dedicated time to yourself. This can be as nourishing as taking regular exercise or eating fresh food daily. It is time out from the rush of daily life. It is a place where you can be purely selfish and spend time with yourself and for yourself.

Bender (2001) examines the value of spending time with yourself:

> Solitude is a state of being that fosters contemplation about what is at the bottom of our minds and in our hearts. It is a state in which a wide variety of feelings come to inform us about our lives and those of others that we are concerned about. (p.6)

Bender goes on to say that through journal writing 'you begin to experience how enjoying minutes and even some hours of solitude on a regular basis makes you sturdier and more effective in dealing with your life' (p.7).

Journal writing provides you with an opportunity for self-expression that is often denied in other arenas. You can express opinions that are unethical, unfair or not politically correct, allowing you to blow off steam and say what should not be said in public. The effect of such an emotional outburst is often cathartic and, if reflected on, it can awaken insights about what needs to be changed in thinking or action. Writing about what you have experienced can help clarify it and put it into context.

Intellectually it can be stimulating to write, and it stretches and improves the memory when it is done regularly. It can increase observational skills and awareness of the senses, which in turn will benefit clinical practice. The writing style becomes more fluid while frequent rereading develops the skills of critical thinking.

Transformation through writing a narrative journal is proportional to the amount of self that you put into the journal. A factual logbook is a useful record but it does not encourage you to explore yourself. A narrative journal entry followed by self-questioning provides the opportunity for insight and change. It invites rereading and provides an interesting record of previous thoughts and feelings. In rereading it you can observe patterns in your life, and notice the recurrence of similar experiences or relationships. It becomes clear whether you met challenges in the same way or with a different attitude.

Considering the advantages of journal writing, it is the purpose of this book to encourage you to begin a journal or expand on what you are already doing. Anything that makes journal writing into a chore will produce resistance and decrease the amount you do it. It is my aim to inspire you into trying out something new, having fun and taking the boredom out of journal writing. In the rest of this chapter there are suggestions about different techniques that can be used in writing a journal. None of them is better than the others, and all of them are given to you as possibilities that might suit you or stimulate your own ideas. In each section there are short reflective exercises that you can experiment with or trawl through for ideas. There is a journal example for clarification and inspiration.

My suggestion is that you experiment and play with some of the exercises that inspire you. If, in reading through each section, you come up with your own ideas about what will suit you, that is even better – try them out!

Recording observations and making descriptions

A journal can be used to record observations or make descriptions. The two could be interchangeable, or we might say that an observation is noticing something specific about a person, place or event, while a description is a wider engagement with the subject. Using the journal to record observations of patients or clients can be quite insightful, especially if you reflect on why you chose to write about them in one way instead of another.

Referring back to the different functions of the two sides of the brain, descriptions appeal to both left- and right-brained writers. Descriptions can be made in a factual, linear way or creatively and expansively. After writing a description you can add a reflection about how much you kept to the facts and how much you wanted to change or embellish the story. Watch out for your inner justifier who will want to say you have just recorded the facts without putting anything of yourself into the description.

Exercise 1
Think back to your earliest memories. What is the first childhood home that you can remember? Take some time remembering it. You will probably find your memory is quite distorted, remembering clearly the rooms you spent most time in, and having blanks about other areas. Your own personal height at the time will have an influence on how big your family home appeared to be. Try to remember colours and textures – in particular, what you liked or disliked.

When you have reconnected to as many memories as you can, decide how you would like to describe this in your journal. Would you write from the point of view of your adult self, or would you write from your childhood perspective? What would influence your choice? Do you want to include a drawing or a map? If so, why? Have fun in describing your childhood home. Afterwards reflect on why you chose to make the description in this way, and what it tells you about your learning style.

Exercise 2

Choose someone you know reasonably well and write a descriptive portrait of them in your journal. Consider carefully before you start and choose someone whom you feel affectionate towards, and whom you can write about with a kind heart. Apart from the slim chance that the person could read what you have written, writing vindictively can actively influence the real-life relationship detrimentally. Bearing this in mind, writing about someone you know is a valuable exercise, and often an enlightening experience.

Begin writing from the left brain and include facts, statistics, numbers, lists and details. For example, you might write about the person's age, size, colouring, career choice, address or family background. Keep your language accurate and to the point.

When you have listed as many of the factual details as you want, start writing from the right brain, using creative descriptions, intuitive suggestions and emotional reactions. Allow your language to be expressive, and, if you wish, write about yourself in relation to this person. Your description will start to evoke the personality or character of your acquaintance. Finally, begin to make connections between the factual description and the creative description, and see what arises.

After you have finished, reflect on whether you were more comfortable writing from the left brain or the right brain.

JOURNAL EXAMPLE

My aunt is a grey-haired lady of 53 who lives with my uncle in a big four-bedroom house in Redstone. She is taller than most women at nearly six foot, and has remained quite slim. She has a large nose and intelligent, pale blue eyes, and she wears reading glasses around her neck on a gold chain. Her undyed grey hair has not been styled for years, but she ties it back with a neat clip. She works in the local school as a counsellor, and, until recently, she would cycle the six miles to get there.

I have never met anyone who is as confident as my aunt. She is an extrovert and expresses her opinions with strength and conviction. She is completely individual, certainly eccentric, and simply does not care what other people think. One evening last summer we went to the theatre, and decided to take the bus back home. My aunt cut past the crowd of people waiting at the bus stop and peered into the adjacent rubbish bin to pull out a newspaper. She said with a big smile to everyone, 'I am a print-aholic. I must be reading something. Look at this newspaper; it's hardly been opened!'

She is not in the least bothered by fashion, but she has a large wardrobe of interesting clothes, bought mainly from charity shops. She chooses autumnal tones and earthy shades, and interesting textures like crushed velvet and tweed. My uncle buys her jewellery made from gemstones, coral and amber, which she wears if she remembers to get it out of the box. Some of her clothes could be decades old. One evening, we went out for a meal, and the dark green silk blouse that she was wearing suddenly shredded across her back as she stretched across the table to reach for the bread. She and my uncle just laughed.

In writing this, I start to wonder what the kids at school think of her. I can't imagine how she works as a counsellor with teenagers. Do they laugh at her behind her back? Do they mock her for her weird, unfashionable clothes? But thinking of her calm manner, unfazed by anything, and her bright intelligent eyes, I'm beginning to see what a wonderful role model she is, teaching the teenagers to confidently tread their own path.

REFLECTIONS

I was a bit bored with the statistical description and moved on to the creative bit as soon as possible. I found I wanted to exaggerate and make her even more eccentric than she is. I wanted to make fun of her, laugh at her a little bit, probably because I get embarrassed by her old clothes when they fall apart, or when she digs into rubbish bins. I projected my need to laugh at her onto the students. The realisation that she could be a role model rather than a figure of fun was quite an eye-opener for me.

The learning journal

A learning journal is more than a memo of things that have been studied, such as books, lectures, lab experiments, field trips, clinics and so on. It becomes a learning journal when you reflect on what you have learned, including your emotional or intellectual reaction to all the stimulating input. This can inform your further studies and become part of self-directed learning.

Andragogy or self-directed learning encourages students to take active responsibility for their own learning. Knowles (1973), writing in *The Adult Learner*, argues that adult learners need a 'sense of discovery':

> ...a sense of frontiersmanship can be cultivated and restored, that the adventure and wonder of life can be renewed, if not increased. If to his self expectation as a continuing learner, an adult could add a picture of himself as one continuing to discover, he could heighten his ability to learn and inquire. (p.168)

The learning journal can be an effective part of self-directed learning. It is a place where you can record fresh insights or new information and make connections to previous knowledge. You can interact with the new information in order to absorb it through thoughts and feelings. Coming to your own conclusion will encourage you to follow up new ideas and expand your learning in new directions. Rereading helps to consolidate your learning.

Some courses — for example online, distance learning courses — include a mandatory study journal that has to be filled in by the students, who receive feedback from the course tutor. This type of journal can contain discussions about the study material, or it can display the skills being learned such as self-reflection or critical thinking. However, the disadvantage of this is that the students can simply present what they think their tutor wants to see. It is another reason for them to modify the narrative. In effect, this can take them away from self-directed learning and back to teacher-directed learning. Moon (2006) writes in *Learning Journals*, 'If journals are to be seen by tutors, then strategic or perceptive students will modify their accounts of observed events to suit what they perceive to be the criteria for assessment' (p.15).

If the learning journal is introduced to the students with a variety of suggestions on how it could be used, and then handed over to them to use it as they will, it can be a valuable part of the self-directed learning. Tutor feedback can be used to support, challenge or to simply add to the learning. See the art journal (Chapter 6) as a further example of the learning journal.

Exercise 1

A personal memory intrudes as I start to write this exercise. When I was at college, I was always impressed that a good friend of mine used to carry around a very large ring binder of notes. One day I asked him whether he was good at rereading his notes, and he laughed guiltily. 'Oh, these are my wife's cookery notes. I don't normally take any notes, but I felt I ought to be carrying a ring binder because everyone else does.'

Write about your own experiences at school, college or university in your journal. Think back to how you recorded information at that time. Were you like many people, simply copying the lecturer's words onto paper? With the benefit of hindsight, would you have gained more if you had reflected on each lecture afterwards?

Exercise 2

Remember your first day at college or the beginning of a conference or seminar. Describe what you observed and what you learned, as well as giving your personal reactions to the material.

JOURNAL EXAMPLE

I had my first study day at college yesterday. It began with an introduction from the principal, a quietly spoken, serious man who told us about the high standards he expected of himself and us. He described himself as a perfectionist, and wanted us to aim high as well. By the time we graduate, we will be treating members of the public, with their health and well-being in our hands. We should always aim towards giving them the best possible service, he told us. It is our responsibility to work towards this goal in the next three years, with the objective of continuously refining our skills, knowledge and experience, for the benefit of ourselves, our clients and our profession.

'If you are not entering this course with the sincere intention of working hard and making the best of your time with us, then I suggest that you leave now,' he said. 'If you have the intention and the commitment to work hard, then you will be successful both in graduating from our college and in creating a fulfilling career for yourself.'

He went on to say:

'This is a distance learning programme, which allows complete flexibility about where or when you do your studies, but creates its own problems in the isolation of all students. I want you to support each other throughout the month between study days, either face to face or on the internet.'

He put us into small groups to discuss how we could help each other, and then put all 16 of us into one big group to create what he called 'a working agreement'. He reminded us that contracts or working agreements are common in many spheres of life; the business contract, the marriage certificate, the prenuptial and the home–school agreement are all different forms of contract, as well as the practitioner–patient agreement. As a group of students going through the college together, having our own agreement would establish ground rules, which in turn would create trust and benefit our learning.

REFLECTIONS

I was rather irritated by the principal with his high standards. I wanted to use the word 'pompous' when I was writing about him. I felt indignant when he said we should commit to working hard or leave now. We don't know what's around the corner, and most of us are mature students with other commitments in life as well. (Is this my inner justifier pre-paving the way for me not to work so hard?)

I took brief notes of what he said, but I've reconstructed these back into his full speech again. Is this really what he said? My impression was that it was all very black-and-white, but now I'm beginning to wonder if it really was that harsh. Certainly my expectations of going back into college after so many years included a feeling of going back to junior school – being treated like ignorant children. Was I expecting the principal to be headmaster-ish? Maybe he was just shy.

Some of the other students seemed irritated at being told that we have to support each other, as if it would drain their energy. But in my mind it will be reciprocal and I'm quite excited by the thought.

I was fascinated by the concept of the working agreement, which I hadn't come across before. But it makes sense. I began to wonder if I could apply it to other situations. The first time Pete and I went on holiday together we ended up arguing because we had completely different expectations. An agreement about what we wanted from the holiday, before we went, would have clarified all that.

Writing to someone specific

There can be great therapeutic value in writing a letter that is not intended to be sent. The letter could be written to a person, such as a client, patient or colleague. It could be written to an institution or a governing body. You can take the opportunity to say the unspeakable to the other person, and the expression of the emotion can be very cathartic. Be aware that writing negatively to another person on a frequent basis can serve to entrench bad feeling through self-justification and damage the relationship even further – but the opposite is also true. Writing positively or affectionately to someone about your happy memories can make you appreciate them more and enhance the relationship.

Another purpose of the unsent letter is that it can help you clarify what you would like to say to someone the next time you meet. I suggested this for a woman who was grieving for her sister, recently diagnosed with cancer. I recommended that in her unsent letter she reminded her sister of her strengths and positive characteristics, including happy memories and times of physical health.

Unsent letters can be written to yourself or parts of yourself. They can be used as a way of giving love and appreciation to yourself, especially in times of trouble. For example, they can be used during times of illness or trauma, to build up the self-confidence and focus on the positive aspects and healing. Once again, it is not advisable to write very much about the illness from a negative stance, because this can cement feelings of no hope and no cure.

At a later time you can reread what you have written, and notice the tone of your letter as well as the specific words that you have used. These can help you gain insights, often giving you hints about what you can do to change or benefit the relationship with yourself or another.

Exercise 1

Think of the last time you were on holiday and remember the sights, sounds, smells, tastes and feeling of being there. Write in your journal as if you're sending a group email to those family and friends who were not on holiday with you. Imagine the email will be read by everyone including your granny and your little brother. Afterwards reflect on what you chose to keep in, and what you left out.

Exercise 2

Think of one of your least favourite patients, the one who makes your heart sink. This is the patient to whom you find it difficult to relate in the clinic. Write an unsent letter to the person, expressing your frustration and allowing yourself to say what is not working between you. Finish your letter with a couple of sentences of appreciation for the patient. Put your letter to one side for a few hours or days and then reread it. Reflect on what you observe and notice if you are changing the story.

JOURNAL EXAMPLE

Dear Bernadette,

You have been coming to me for homeopathic treatment for six months, and I don't feel we are making much progress. I feel there are hidden agendas that I don't understand.

I was shocked when you came for your first appointment, with a carrier bag full of notebooks about your symptoms that you expected me to read. I felt irritated because it seemed as if you were setting me extra homework, when I was already working hard on your behalf. I hope this didn't show on my face and that I politely refused. At every subsequent appointment you read out from your notebook all the minutiae of your physical symptoms, in the manner of dictation. You're very resistant to talking spontaneously about your moods and feelings and it is very difficult for me to get a holistic picture to make a prescription. It is as if you use all the minutiae to keep us on a very superficial level. I wonder if you're afraid of going deeper.

You have been to several homeopaths in the past and you have said that none of them have helped you. I wonder if you are a therapy hopper, refusing to give us enough information to work on and then blaming us for failure.

When you first came to see me, I explained carefully about the homeopathic process, and I gave you a couple of leaflets to read. I told you that the choice of remedy depends upon my understanding of your mental, emotional and physical make-up. With homeopathy, we always prescribe on the individual, not on the disease diagnosis. I need to understand your character, to find out what differentiates you from other people with the same problems.

I feel helpless because sometimes you are pushing my boundaries, giving me more and more minutiae with all the details of what you had for breakfast and when you went to the toilet – and yet at other times you're putting up strong boundaries, preventing me from getting the information I need.

I have tried prescribing on my observations such as your anxiety about your health and your need to document all the small symptoms. You have reported some improvements, but it is clear to me that there has not been a significant change and I'm not satisfied with my prescriptions. Are we just going to keep on like this, until you move on to join another practitioner? I would rather not waste your time. I think it is better that I tell you honestly I cannot help you any more.

I appreciate the time that you brought me daffodils from your garden. But now that I think about it, wasn't that another pushing of the boundaries? Was it a little sweetener so that I will go on listening to minutiae?

I appreciate your rare smile, and I appreciate that time I looked out of my window and saw you had arrived early, and were taking the time to stroke my cat who was sunning himself on the wall.

I'm sorry that I haven't been able to help you more, and I wish you all the best for the future.

Yours, etc.

REFLECTIONS

It was a relief to express all my anger and frustration with this patient. I am aware there is some complex game going on, of her being desperately anxious about her health but at the same time having an investment in remaining in the same familiar place. She won't talk about her relationship with her husband – and that might (or might not) be the root of the problem.

Writing the letter also helped me see that she has her own strengths and she is not as vulnerable as I originally perceived. In fact when I look at the drama triangle, I frequently go into the role of Victim when I'm with her, and I perceive her as Persecutor. I wanted to self-justify by blaming her for being a therapy hopper.

While writing the letter I wanted to emphasise the fact that I had explained to Bernadette very carefully about the homeopathic case-taking process, but I probably skipped through it in reality, assuming that as she had been to so many other homeopaths she would understand. Maybe before I give up on her entirely, I could renegotiate about how we spend the consultations. No more notebooks for a start!

Outpouring of emotions

Some journal writers aim to present a true and honest record, like an accurate photograph of events. But as we have seen, most people allow their unconscious thoughts, attitudes, wishes and needs to influence the way they write, distorting the original history into a more palatable or more critical version.

The clinic can be a place where the practitioner experiences strong emotion. This can be from a patient's sad story, through witnessing a patient weeping or expressing other emotions, or because the practitioner's own issues have been triggered. Some practitioners have methods to cleanse themselves of a patient's atmosphere on a regular basis, such as lighting a candle or opening the door and window. Some patients' stories seem to adhere more than others. Sometimes just talking about the case with a colleague, critical friend or supervisor is enough. When they aren't available, though, the journal becomes the perfect outlet.

It can be immensely cathartic to use the journal as a forum for discharging emotion. The inability of the journal to answer back provides comfort and collusion. The emotional discharge acts like a purge, leaving you clean, empty and energised to face the real world again. As Rainer (1978) reminds us:

> The importance of the diary in these cases is not as a product – a point I can't repeat too often – but in the life that is freed from excessive anger, confusion and grief. Putting the pain in the diary keeps it from destroying a life. The life liberated from such destructive emotions is the true 'product' of this purgative process. (p.54)

However, if the journal is continually used to express anger, grief, frustration or disappointment, it can entrench you in the negative emotion, cutting you off from personal insights and self-development. If you have the opportunity to write about hopeful, optimistic, happy or loving feelings, then seize it.

Exercise 1

This exercise might suit someone who finds it difficult to express their emotions. Choose a situation where you felt unhappy with what was going on; for example, a situation where you felt disturbed and uncomfortable, but couldn't identify what emotion was behind the feeling. First of all, reassure yourself that you don't need to name the emotion. Then find a metaphor that will describe the feeling – for instance, feeling run over by a snowplough, feeling like an athlete who has just run a marathon, feeling like a kite that has broken its string and been taken away by the wind, or feeling like a snail hiding inside its shell.

Write this metaphor in your journal as a title, and then write a description of what happened. As you write your description, consciously refer to the metaphor and extend it. Reflect on what you have discovered.

Exercise 2
Choose a situation where you felt indignant, angry, saddened or embarrassed – for example, an event that happened while you were travelling to work, an encounter with a manager at work, or the passing away of a very sick patient. Write a short description of this in your journal, allowing yourself to be completely emotional in what you write, using vivid adjectives and emphatic comments. Afterwards, reflect on what that felt like.

Exercise 3
Remember a situation where you felt extraordinarily happy and elated – for example, when you had just won a prize, fallen in love, bought your first car, achieved your sporting goal, or graduated from college or university. Begin with writing about your fantastic experience, and express as clearly as possible your feelings of delight and joy. Then add to this with a list of other smaller, happy experiences – for example, when you were observing a beautiful sunset, taking exercise, talking to a good friend, hugging a child, or cooking a delicious meal. Enjoy all your happy memories as you write about them, feeling your mood rising up to happiness again.

Afterwards reflect on how easy or difficult it was to write only about positive, happy and delightful things.

Here are two journal examples showing how an outpouring of emotion can be negative or positive.

JOURNAL EXAMPLE

It was cold today, and I was cold, wet and thoroughly pissed off before I even got to work. I woke up in the night feeling chilled but I was too sleepy to find an extra blanket.

Hot coffee didn't help much and outside my face was blasted with freezing rain. At the corner the road was flooded, same as last year – the roads committee are all concrete-headed bastards, they never do any work. A driver went through the lake too fast sending a fan of freezing, muddy water over me. I shouted out curses and made several expressive hand gestures, but he just drove on.

By the time I got to the station, I had had enough and felt furious that I had to stand on the platform with the miserable, bedraggled crowd. They had no right to grumble when they had probably all got a lift to the station.

The train took ages to come and when it arrived it was already quite full and smelled like a wet dog. There was standing room only and the windows were steamed up. The train lurched as we moved out of the station and an overweight man was thrown against me. I spent several moments grimly fantasising about wearing stilettos so that I could stamp on his feet, or having a hidden knife tucked in the base of my handbag in the manner of a secret agent. His large wet overcoat was disgusting. I turned away, only to find a woman's umbrella was dripping onto my foot. I consigned her to four weeks of community service, and that was just her first charge. If her behaviour was offensive in any other way, it would go up to eight weeks.

The train clunked into the next station, and although only two got off it looked like 20 were trying to get on. Mr Bright and Breezy was one of them, singing along to his music. There should be a law against people who sing on trains first thing in the morning.

REFLECTIONS

Whew! I clearly did a lot of exaggerating when I wrote this, but it was fun saying all those horrible things, and I feel so much better having done it!

Here is a more cheerful journal example.

JOURNAL EXAMPLE

I ran my first workshop today and it went really well! I'm so excited! Dear diary, you wouldn't believe how nervous I was this morning. The workshop wasn't until 11 a.m., but the time passed in a rush with me checking and double-checking that I had everything with me and then having to rush to the bathroom...

I got there in plenty of time and started setting up my stuff, and seven people arrived, just the right number! I kind of relaxed when I saw there wasn't going to be a big crowd intimidating me. I got everyone to sit in a circle, introduced myself and got them to introduce themselves. They were really nice people, open, friendly and interested. Most of them were young mums with kids at school, but two were retired ladies, alert and enquiring. Just the sort of people I'd wanted to come!

I felt I was talking very well and could explain things without hesitation, especially in the question-and-answer session. They asked really interesting questions. The time just flew by and I found I had prepared more than was necessary – but better that way round than not having enough stuff to teach. Eventually the caretaker had to ask us to leave, which was really funny. Everyone took my flyer and my business cards. I think I might have got several new patients out of the workshop. Isn't that great? That's exactly the outcome I wanted!

Now that I've got all my workshop materials organised, I feel full of enthusiasm to try another one. It feels like a great way of setting up my business and filling my clinic with new patients. I might even set up regular classes – wow, I can't believe I just wrote that! I always used to say that I would never become a teacher!

Dear diary, I am so pleased that today went so well. I was so lucky to have the chance to run a mini-workshop. I really appreciated being asked! The people who came were lovely and I learned a lot from them, especially the wise old ladies! Roll on the next one!

REFLECTIONS

While writing about it I was aware that I wanted to bask in the feelings of success, so that it became an experience that I could refer back to. I found myself deliberately using a very excited and enthusiastic writing style, so that I can recreate my pleasure in my first workshop, any time I reread my journal.

Explore your own mythology

Writers have been fascinated by the non-human and superhuman in myth, legend, folklore or, more recently, science fiction. When writing about humans, they are limited by human ability, but the non-human imposes no limitation on the imagination. Human characteristics can be exaggerated, perverted or reversed. Myths are a form of traditional story, often developed by ancient tribes as a way of understanding the world and how it began. They are peopled with passionate, emotional gods of uncertain temper, or glossy superheroes – and occasionally weak or faulty humans. The characters of folklore are wizards, elves, ogres, sprites, fairies, witches and so on.

Modern folklore arises easily and spontaneously. For example, in a student clinic one supervisor will be called a dragon, while another will be called a pussycat. Patients who return regularly to the student clinic will get labelled all too easily as 'nice', 'easy to work with', 'always complains', 'incurable' or 'has awful children'. My personal experience was after working with a family for four or five years, when I overheard the child who answered the phone shout, 'Mummy, it's the witch on the phone.'

Even stronger than the mythology made up about other people is the mythology that you make up about yourself. For example, many people feel they have a skills deficiency, which is something that is put aside as an impossible task rather than accepted as something that just hasn't been learned yet – for example, 'I'm no good with computers', 'I couldn't help a patient with this or that pathology', or 'I'm hopeless at charging fees.'

If you take the time to write down one of these myths and then question it, it can be surprising how often it is simply an excuse not to do something perceived at the outset to be difficult or boring.

Exercise 1

Choose one of your negative myths, one that has been with you for a long time. Start off with the words 'I can't' or 'I'm no good at'. You will probably have a strong attachment to this myth, and find yourself saying, 'But it's true!' Using reflective questions, challenge yourself, asking:

- What do I gain from being unable to do this thing?
- How do I view myself being unable to do it?
- How do others view me when I can't do it?
- Am I prepared to change?

Exercise 2

Imagine a patient who has changed practitioners within one clinic or within a small community. The patient's notes are transferred to the new practitioner and they appear innocuous. However, an underlying message comes with this patient, either encoded in the notes or through a brief comment from the previous practitioner. The underlying message is the mythology about this patient's level of understanding, compliance, autonomy or even appreciation of the practitioner's service.

Write about the mythology from the practitioner's point of view, and then from the patient's point of view. Notice who you sympathise with.

Exercise 3

See how easy it is to create a new mythology. Start with writing a description of a familiar scene in order to loosen up your writing style, and, after a couple of paragraphs or a page, allow reality to give way to fantasy. Begin to push the boundaries of rational description, and enter into your imagination. Notice what appeals to you and whether you want an abrupt changeover from one style to the other, or whether you prefer a gentle amalgamation.

JOURNAL EXAMPLE

On Sunday morning I woke up early to see sunshine and blue skies, glorious after a week of grey English clouds and rain. I showered and had a quick breakfast, restless with longing for the fresh air in my lungs and the warmth of the sun on my face. I put Honey on the lead and we walked briskly through the streets of suburban terraces to get to the river, where the trees are ancient and traffic cannot be heard.

The water was quite high in the river and, standing for a moment on the arched wooden footbridge, I could see it rippling and catching at the banks with flashes of reflected sunshine and blue sky in each little wave, like a crowd of silver fish jostling to get downstream. The trees, after a week of rain, looked fresh and bright under their canopy of green.

Honey, who had run ahead, turned and stopped in puzzlement, trying to assess whether she should return to me; so after a few minutes of pleasurable observation, I walked on, following the wooded path beside the river. The sunshine glinted through the trees making patterns on the path, and as we came up towards the weir the sound of the water grew louder. Here the current was stronger, leaping over the concrete step of the weir, creating a smooth glossy curve down to the water below.

Leaving the weir behind, the path came out of the woods onto a fine green meadow, where the grasses and wildflowers were stretching up towards the sun. The sound of gentle bells caught my attention, and I turned to see a slow progression of healers and medicants walking solemnly towards the river. It was the day of their early summer ceremony, I realised with surprise and awe. They were dressed in sparkling white robes and some had flowers or herbs twisted into their hair. Each held an intricate flagon made out of gold and purple glass, which they were going to fill with holy water from the river. They gathered at the river's edge, and carefully washed their hands and feet, while singing and throwing flowers into the water. Then one by one they walked slowly across the river, feeling their way with bare feet and murmuring blessings and incantations. At the very centre of the current, they each stooped gracefully and filled their flask.

I had sunk down in the grass to watch, motioning to Honey that she should lie down next to me. The beauty of the morning, the fresh sunshine, the wild flowers, the sparkling robes and the murmured ceremony filled my heart with peace and hope. Very few people are privileged to watch the healers' ceremony, and I felt deeply moved. Observed over thousands of years, it has always taken place on a different day during the summer, in a different part of the river. It is said that each part of the ritual is symbolic of the healer's understanding of disease and spiritual growth. It is said that those who watch the ceremony receive a blessing and a spiritual cleansing.

REFLECTIONS

I enjoyed writing this story immensely. It starts off with someone who just wants to get out into nature after a week of rain, then jumps into mythology with the healers' ceremony. This felt right to me. As a Reiki practitioner and healer myself, I know the importance of cleansing yourself and allowing healing just to flow through you – like the current in the river. I like rituals; they are significant marker posts. While I was writing the story, I was clear that I didn't want the ceremony just to be limited to healers so I included 'medicants' to include anyone who is in the health professions.

I'm interested that I cast myself as an observer rather than one of the healers taking part in the ceremony. I wonder why? It is as if I am reluctant to take my place among the qualified or the professionals, seeing myself still as a student with hope for the future. I'm a bit shy about joining the ranks of wise women and wise men. I think it would be useful for me to create a little ritual or ceremony, to congratulate myself on graduating. I, too, have walked across the river and filled my flask with holy water.

Creating poetry

Poetry has a different cadence and tempo from other forms of writing. The pulse of the poem is carefully chosen and often tightly controlled. Words are chosen specifically for the imagery they invoke, and for the sound and mouth-feel of the pronunciation. How each word sits next to the following word is considered, and double meanings or metaphors are enjoyed. In previous centuries there were patterns or formulas in which poems could be written, and rhymes were usually expected. Nowadays rhythm is frequently chosen instead of rhyme and there is immense flexibility of style.

Writing a short poem about a client, patient or experience can make you put a different value on it. You will see it in a different light, and again it will be interesting to notice what you choose to put in and what you choose to leave out.

Exercise 1

Think back to a patient seen in clinic who caused an emotional reaction in you. Perhaps it was the sadness of their story, or perhaps their strong emotion that resonated with you for some other reason. Without trying to rationalise or understand what happened and why it happened, sit with the feeling for a while and then see if you can construct a poem about that feeling. In this exercise, the aim is to move from emotion into poetry via intuition – in other words, to remain on the right side of the brain without trying to be rational or logical. Allow the poem to defuse the emotion for you.

Exercise 2

Remember a time when you were feeling overworked or overwhelmed. Design a small ritual for yourself in order to leave all the work behind you and simply relax. For example, lying in a warm bath in the candlelight, going for a walk, clearing up your desk and throwing away old papers, or slowly and lovingly preparing a meal. Write a poem about your experience of your ritual cleansing from all the stress.

JOURNAL EXAMPLE

WALKING

Walking briskly across chill and misty fields,
The diffused brightness of the lemon sun,
Gives a freshness to autumn's first frosts.

My cluttered desk cried out wait, don't go!
But the sweeping fields refresh my soul,
Tired from endless, grey people talking.

A fox in my path in gold and russet coat,
Pauses to watch me in quiet contemplation,
Sharing a moment of infinite peace.

A joyful robin in the tree with scarlet berries,
Bursts into song, a bright tale of hope,
My spirit flies free and I am healed.

(Wood 2011)

REFLECTIONS

There are several different experiences rolled into this poem, but they were all times of escape from my desk, and they were all healing experiences after being too busy in clinic. It's interesting that I saw my clients as 'endless, grey people', because in reality I really enjoy being with them. Seeing them as grey and endless points towards burn-out, and makes it all the more important that I take downtime to refresh my soul, and become healed by nature.

CHAPTER 4

ESSENTIAL TOOLS FOR REFLECTIVE JOURNALS

Late summer
long shadows on the grass
quiet reflection

Self-reflection can be described as an ongoing process of regular, deliberate investigation into issues that arise from experience. The purpose is to explore the inner motivations, attitudes, beliefs or assumptions in order to increase self-knowledge and make appropriate changes for the future. The issue can be chosen because it was experienced, it was observed or because it arose through studying theory.

Honest self-reflection leads to self-improvement, which enhances both professional and personal life. Johns (2009) takes this even further. He writes in *Becoming a Reflective Practitioner*:

> I want to emphasise that reflection is always action orientated towards realising vision as a lived reality. In other words, reflection is not a neutral thing but a political and cultural movement towards creating a better, more caring and humane world. (p.16)

Reflection can take place before, during or after action. Before the event, options are considered and plans are made; during the event, minor or major adjustments are continuously made in relation to what is perceived; and afterwards there is a process of looking back and learning from the event. The first and last of these can be done using the reflective journal as a form of 'reflection *on* action' – while 'reflection *in* action' happens in the heat of the moment.

I am a firm believer that everyone can self-reflect if they want to, and the more it is practised the better it gets. In saying this, it is important to separate the act of self-reflection from the ability to write smoothly and coherently. Self-reflection will happen when there is an intention to investigate experience, whether it is discussed orally, written about or expressed creatively.

Working with the reflective journal

The self-reflective journal is of great value in the health and caring professions, where practitioners need to identify their own issues in order to help the client or patient in an unprejudiced and balanced way. It gives space and opportunity to process new experiences and information, to review established work patterns or to make changes for the future. Used regularly, it supports, nourishes, challenges and develops critical thinking.

As head of practitioner development running a distance learning homeopathy college on the internet, I decided that a mandatory part of the course would be that each student would fill in an online reflective journal every week. I wanted them to get into the habit of self-reflection and decided not to grade this work but simply give feedback. I gave the students an open choice about whether they reflected on their personal life, their work or their studies.

Students who joined the college in the first few years found this a very tough assignment, being unused to self-reflection and disliking the fact that it was being read. Gradually, it became an accepted part of the course and individual resistance was replaced by acceptance and then appreciation. At various times throughout the training, I asked the students to reflect on their learning. One student wrote:

> My greatest learning is the self-reflective journal. I wrote the self-reflective journal every week and I found my attitude as a practitioner changed. This will help me very much in the future. For the last half year I have noticed many changes.
>
> Formerly I was eager to cure my clients. However, I noticed recently that when I'm really keen to cure the client, they become uncomfortable when I show this. I reflected on it and realised it is necessary to get rid of my deep attachment to the client

getting better. It is much better when I have a free feeling, and don't try to persuade the client to change their lifestyle. This allows them to be free, and they may change through their own choice. (personal communication)

This brief example shows how an observation can be taken into self-reflection, and after due consideration a change made in the practitioner's attitude, leading to further reflection. Self-reflection will frequently go in cycles like this.

The reflective journal can be used for many different aspects of your work – for example, to:

- review aspects of your work, and assess your strengths and weaknesses

- learn from your experiences in order to provide a better service for others

- explore a specific incident in order to understand it at a deeper level

- expand your thinking to gain a wider viewpoint

- observe your emotions and make links to other emotional responses you have had

- explore the past and present in order to make action plans for the future

- build up your self-confidence.

This is a tentative list of some of the uses of the reflective journal, focusing on practitioners who are just beginning self-reflection. See the next chapter for the extended list applying to the experienced reflector. I'm aware that this division into novice and experienced will be useful for those who like to move forward slowly and steadily, but could prove irritating for those who do not like limitations or boundaries imposed upon them. As with the whole of this book, feel free to pick and choose what is going to suit you or what might stretch you.

Transformation through self-reflection

In the self-reflective journal, issues are worked on as they arise. For some people, reflection can be difficult at first, especially if there are habits of self-criticism or self-justification. But after a while keeping a journal becomes very empowering because as you understand yourself better, your ability to change and redirect the future increases. Keeping a regular journal has an impact on your self-development, your relationships with clients and colleagues, your pride in your work and your professionalism. Moon (2006) calls this being 'at the wheel', in her book, *Learning Journals*:

> The essential nature of journal-writing means that – to use a metaphor – the writer is at the wheel and is steering... For the writer, writing of the journal provides a focusing point, an opportunity to order thoughts...and to make sense of a situation or of information. (p.27)

Your critical thinking will improve. This is the ability to investigate impartially, think independently and draw conclusions. Critical thinking is rational, logical, objective, systematic and works mainly with the left brain. Taylor (2000) suggests that the attitudes necessary for critical thinking include 'thinking independently, intellectual humility, courage, empathy, integrity, and perseverance' (p.15).

Working with the emotions can feel uncomfortable at first, and you might find you have some resistance. However, over time, you will learn to acknowledge your emotions, and not judge them. You will write from a more conscious position, observing yourself and noticing emotions, appreciating them for what they are without being self-critical. There will be a sense of release and unburdening.

The self-reflective journal gives you the opportunity to make links with the past. If you react to something in a particularly strong or uncharacteristic way, it might be because it is triggering one of your prejudices or fixed beliefs. Fixed beliefs often arise from childhood and include unconscious moral judgements about yourself and others. They can be expressed as absolutes such as 'they are', 'they should', 'I have to', 'I can't' and 'you ought'. Self-reflection can help you reframe some of these beliefs and discard others. You can create new attitudes, values and beliefs that are no longer childhood borrowings but your own considered adult decisions.

If you make regular entries in the journal, it can give you an effective overview of your work and abilities. Writing about your own strengths is an opportunity to have a quiet boast about what you did well, and will consolidate good working practice and increase your confidence. Writing about your weaknesses does not mean entering into an orgy of self-criticism. It is simply an opportunity to explore what happened, why it happened and how you can make changes in the future.

Experience can be widened and self-awareness increased through using and rereading the journal. Relationships with family, friends, colleagues, clients or patients become easier as you get more choices about how to deal with other people. As you begin to understand your own attitudes and expectations of others, you can decide if these are appropriate, and either change them or explain them to others. The other people will know where they stand, and the relationship will become simpler and easier.

Finding a journal style that suits you

There are no rules about how you should do your self-reflective journal. As with the other journals discussed in this book, the aim is self-knowledge rather than perfection of writing style, and you can write on paper or on your computer. An awareness of your preferred learning style can inform your technique or journaling style (see Chapter 2). If you choose to write on paper, it might be advisable to use a bound notebook so that you won't be tempted to tear pages out in an editorial storm. Alternatively, if you want to write on whatever paper is to hand, you can discipline yourself to file every reflective page. If you keep your messy, hesitant pages, they will tell you a lot when you are rereading your journal.

Try to get into the habit of writing regularly in your journal. It is a commitment to yourself that might appear like a chore from the outset, but over time you will definitely benefit from it. Taylor (2000), writing in *Reflective Practice*, compares it to getting regular exercise. Some days you might feel tired and tempted to abandon it, so it will take dedication and determination. Taylor goes on to say:

> After years of practising, teaching and researching reflection, I
> have come to the conclusion it takes some effort, which involves

determination, courage and a sense of humour. Other qualities may be involved in reflection, but it seems to me that these requisites are essential. (p.71)

Each entry in your journal should begin with the date and a description of an experience, issue, dilemma or observation. This sets the scene for the discussion and analysis that follows. I recommend that the description should be brief, so that you don't get entrenched in what happened and you save energy for the reflective work that follows. A longer description can be used for narrative journals. There are numerous ways in which you can reflect, including the methodologies and exercises suggested later. Often, your reflection will end with an action plan, although I have found that a very deep piece of work can produce a change of attitude that initiates change in the outside world without the need of an action plan as such.

Some teachers of self-reflection suggest that you should start a journal entry with a 'critical incident' – for example, something that happened in practice that you reacted to emotionally. I don't use this phrase because it seems (to me) to suggest that the topic for reflection should be something important, serious and weighty. I prefer a more flexible view of self-reflection. You can equally well start with a vague sense of discomfort or the opposite – a feeling of pleasure that you have done a good job with a particular patient or client. You can simply review the past week in practice, or prepare yourself for something new.

You should feel free to change your journaling style and technique, according to the subject you're writing about. I recommend that you experiment with different journal-writing techniques to find out which is the most comfortable and which is the most effective for learning – these are not always the same thing. In trying them out, you can have variety and stimulation, and make informed choices about how to reflect in the future.

In the rest of this chapter there are suggestions about techniques, with exercises and examples to stimulate your desire to get started and excite your imagination. As with the rest of this book, feel free to change or extend the exercises in any way. They are only suggestions, not instructions. Add some reflections after doing each exercise.

Feedback from a critical friend

If you are a novice in self-reflection, you might feel uncertain about what to write, or you might want a reality check about whether you are writing to a deep enough level. In this case, you might find it useful to ask someone to be your critical friend or supervisor for a few weeks or months. However, it is always advisable to create a clear working agreement or contract with the other person before you begin. This is an agreement about how often you will show your reflective pieces, what sort of feedback you want in return, how long this will go on for and how much should be charged. Choose someone that you have a good rapport with, and you can trust and respect. It is better to ask someone with previous experience of self-reflection, even if that experience was only gained in classroom role-plays.

The role of the critical friend is both to support and challenge you. They should listen to or read your reflections in a non-judgemental way, and use gentle questions to make you think further. They are not expected to solve your problems or find answers for you, although if you're really stuck they might point you in a certain direction. Their main task is to encourage you in your own reflective process.

If you are not in a position to receive feedback from a critical friend or supervisor, you could try the second exercise that follows. If you still find it difficult to assess whether you are writing enough in quantity or depth, you could try working from one of the reflective frameworks (see Chapter 7). When you are more confident with the process and have seen the value of the results, you can be more flexible with the methodology.

Exercise 1

Write notes in your journal in preparation for creating a working agreement with a critical friend. Decide how much you will write and how often you will send it to them. Choose what sort of feedback you would like – for example, you might want sandwich feedback (approval followed by critique followed by approval) or an equal balance between support and challenge. You might want feedback in the form of questions or observations, and/or a review at the end of your time together.

Consider any other expectations you might have of your critical friend.

Exercise 2

Write a short reflective piece focusing on the last time someone irritated you at your workplace or college. Begin with the story of what happened, keeping it brief. Then you can investigate it, using some or all of the following questions – you can answer the questions in any order.

- What are the significant issues?
- How do I feel about them?
- What was I trying to achieve?
- What was the other person trying to achieve?
- How does this relate to other similar incidents?
- What sense can I make of it?
- What would I do differently if it happened again?

Leave your reflection for a couple of days without rereading it. When you're ready to return to it, sit down quietly for five minutes, relaxing with long, slow breaths. Call to mind someone you would like to use as a positive role model, such as a supervisor, teacher, relative or manager. Remember this person's tone of voice, and any expressions or catchphrases that they use. After a few minutes, reopen your reflection and read it from the point of view of your role model, giving yourself feedback as that person would have done.

After you have finished, spend some time reflecting on this experience. Then write further notes in your journal about what you have learned.

Exercise 3

If you already have someone who will act as a critical friend or supervisor, write your self-reflection on something you have been doing recently, and send it to them. Copy their feedback into your journal, and do a further reflection on anything that arises for you.

JOURNAL EXAMPLE

I have been thinking a lot about the exercise we did last month at college, choosing picture postcards to represent how we see ourselves as practitioners in the future. I chose four pictures:

- Two women having a discussion over a cup of tea.

- A man standing in an open doorway.

- A gardener with a tray of seedlings.

- A doctor with a stethoscope.

My reasons for these choices were that the man in the doorway welcomes new patients and the gardener nourishes and protects the seedlings. The two women talking showed a sort of intensity but friendliness that I would hope to have as a practitioner. The doctor reminded me of being professional.

I was quite shocked when the tutor suggested that my choices showed a lack of boundaries. She thought I was being too welcoming and, although I have chosen to be a nutritional therapist, I wouldn't need to nourish and protect my patients or I would be denying them their own autonomy and responsibility. It was quite a wake-up call for me. She even questioned whether I really would want to have a 'cup of tea relationship' with a patient.

Looking after Mum has turned me into a carer, so the caring aspect of being a practitioner is very familiar to me. But I don't want my patients to be dependent on me in the way that Mum is. I don't want them to look at me as 'Mummy' either. I want to have a certain amount of distance between me and them, like the picture of the doctor, whose white coat creates a formality and boundary.

Jason (my critical friend) has been encouraging me to add an action plan to my self-reflections. I suppose the question is: How can I be a caring practitioner who has a good relationship with the patients and at the same time create good boundaries?

ACTION PLAN

I don't want to wear a white coat but I could wear smart or formal clothes when I see patients. I will make sure that my work environment looks clean and tidy, even if I'm working from home. I can avoid building up friendships with my patients. I have my own friends already.

FEEDBACK FROM THE CRITICAL FRIEND

Another excellent reflection, with some careful thoughts and analysis. I agree with you that it is healthier as a practitioner to have a certain distance between yourself and your patients. You can be nurturing while they are in your clinic room, but you don't need to nourish them throughout the rest of the week or month. Your action plan is excellent, and you might want to add to it over the coming year.

Let's change the rules about the picture postcards. You can change your cards. Working from memory or from your imagination, choose which postcards you would keep, which you would discard, and which new ones you would pick up. See how that feels.

Thank you, Jason.

REFLECTIONS AFTER FEEDBACK

What fun! I can choose new picture postcards! I would keep the two women talking (although I would remove their cups of tea) and the doctor. I would replace the man in the doorway with a man on the phone with an open diary in front of him. He is booking in new patients. This image feels more professional to me but it is still welcoming patients. I would replace the gardener with a teacher, who is professional, organised and enables other people to learn and become responsible for themselves.

That feels much better! I have learned a lot about boundaries doing this exercise. I will see if I can find some clipart that represents these characters. It will remind me if I have pictures glued into my journal.

Watching a movie

Newcomers to self-reflection can feel as if they are being put into the hot seat, especially if the journal is part of a study assignment and will be read by a tutor. This pressure can increase their emotional attachment to whatever issues they are discussing, making them want to justify their actions and prove themselves right. This is understandable human nature for all who feel they are backed into a corner, but self-justification is not self-reflection. Self-justification keeps the writer in the same place without providing any insights. Self-reflection needs a certain amount of detachment so that the issue is viewed objectively and learning can occur.

If you are a novice to self-reflection, remind yourself that it is not a trial or an examination: it is just an expansion of the original experience. There will always be some aspects of the situation that you could have done better, and there will always be some aspects that you can feel good about.

Stepping back from the original issue and reviewing it as if it is a movie can be an interesting and helpful exercise in being more objective. It can put you into a cooler relationship with the original issue so that there is less attachment and more objective questioning. It allows you to adopt an attitude of gentle curiosity. The three exercises that follow are suggestions about how you might work with viewing an incident as a movie, but, as always, you are encouraged to play with the idea and find something that suits you personally.

Exercise 1

You are going to write about your last weekend. Take a few minutes to remember the household chores that you had to do, the people to whom you spoke and your relaxation or entertainment. Write about a small part of your weekend in the form of a screenplay. Write about yourself as one of the characters in your screenplay using the third person, 'he' or 'she'. Keep as accurately as possible to what happened; don't use your imagination to change history, but use the technique to write about yourself with detachment.

When you have finished, reread what you have written and do some self-reflection, still writing about yourself in the third person. Deliberately include the words, 'That's interesting; I wonder why she/he...'

Exercise 2

Imagine that a documentary film was made about two or three hours of your work in clinic, focusing on an incident from the last few weeks. Choose which incident was filmed for the imaginary documentary and then imagine you are writing for a newspaper, reviewing this film for the arts pages. You are an unusual reviewer, because you are completely neutral and without prejudice!

Once again keep accurately to what happened, and don't change history. Tell yourself the incident has been filmed already and cannot be changed. Begin your review with a brief introduction, explaining what the movie is about; then describe the characters and comment on the interaction.

Exercise 3

Choose an incident that happened to you at work or at home. Write literally as a screenplay for a movie. You can give some of the back story if you feel it is necessary, and you can write the screenplay as a narrative or a series of characters' speeches. If you wish, you can take the role of director and add lighting, camera angles, crowd scenes and so on. Have fun telling the story.

When you have finished, do some self-reflections on what you have learned.

JOURNAL EXAMPLE

This short movie tells the story of a shiatsu practitioner and her client, a young woman. The film begins with very brief clips of the shiatsu practitioner preparing her clinic for the session, and the young woman hurrying up the road. The shiatsu practitioner is doing some meditation and has lit a candle. The young woman is walking faster and faster, almost at a trot, when she trips over a paving stone and falls flat on her face. The next clip shows the practitioner looking at her clock and leaving a message on her client's phone. Then we see the young woman sitting on the bus, with a swollen and bleeding face. Other people on the bus look away. Finally, the disappointed practitioner has blown out the candle and is getting on with some paperwork when her client arrives.

The next scene is set within the clinic. The practitioner is irritable as she goes to answer the door, and doesn't notice the state of the woman. She tells her to come in and sit down, turning away to pick up her notes. The young woman notices the rejecting body language and for her this is the last straw. She starts to tremble all over and asks for a glass of water. The practitioner hears something in the voice, and looks up with surprise, seeing for the first time the cut face and bloodstained tissue.

The startled practitioner goes into overdrive, asking what happened, running around to get water, wet tissues, dry tissues, calendula cream and rescue remedy. The woman starts to cry, and then gets embarrassed with her tears and apologises for being late, for causing trouble, for crying. The practitioner hesitates for a moment, not knowing what to do, and then says firmly, 'tea', and leaves the room to return in a few minutes with two cups of herbal tea.

Sipping tea, the young woman is able to explain why she was late and hurrying, and talk about her experience of being ignored while she sat on the bus with a bleeding face. The practitioner offers a short shiatsu session, which is gratefully accepted.

REFLECTIONS

Here we see a shiatsu practitioner (me) who had a carefully planned routine to prepare for the session, and was quite put out when her client was late. She unconsciously paralleled the rejecting behaviour of the people on the bus, and then overcompensated out of guilt. Leaving the room to make tea was a good opportunity for her to breathe deeply for a few minutes, and get herself back into practitioner mode again. But at the same time leaving the room was abandoning her client just at the point when she needed most sympathy.

I am pleased that the practitioner has clear time boundaries, but it's a shame that she feels resentment towards a client who turns up late. It is good practice that she prepares herself in the room before each treatment, but it is disappointing that she had to leave the room in order to clear her own emotions of resentment and guilt. It is excellent that she has a first-aid kit to hand and that there was still time to offer a short shiatsu session before the next client arrived. In terms of the drama triangle, the patient was the Victim, and the shiatsu practitioner swung between Rescuer and Persecutor.

Strengths and weaknesses

I am a strong advocate of including both positives and negatives in a journal. The self-reflective journal will be a necessary recipient of problems, dilemmas, upsets and failures. It is through working on these issues that a writer can begin to understand themselves and initiate change. If these issues are not brought into the journal, the writer is being superficial and will not claim the reward of self-development. However, if the journal writer is continuously being self-critical, it will lower their self-esteem and make them reluctant to write. In extreme cases, writing about mistakes or failure can induce a vicious circle, encouraging more of the same.

Self-criticism can be a deeply ingrained habit, arising from childhood when a parent's passing angry comment is locked into the child's mind as a truism and becomes part of their life script. These negative habits can hold people back, limiting them from fulfilling a greater potential. I have found that the adult learners on the distance learning course that I teach can be quick to find fault with themselves, frequently ending a self-reflection with the comment, 'I need to study more.' This may be true, but it leaves them in an uncomfortable place where they are more likely to turn their back on studying and seek happiness elsewhere. Feeling cheerful about some aspect of the work that went well is far more likely to attract them to do more studying.

If strengths and weaknesses are both given page space in the journal, the writer feels a sense of balance. All successful outcomes should be recorded, celebrated and explored so that they can be repeated. This could be, for example, the intuitive changes in behaviour and attitude that have come about as a result of reflection in action. It could be new strategies that have been tried out following a previous reflection and action plan. It could be the resolution of difficult ethical or moral situations, or simply when routine work is done with care, positivity, honesty and integrity.

Writing about your successes helps you identify your strengths, boosts your self-confidence and encourages you to repeat successful behaviour. The self-reflective journal should be something that supports you as well as being a learning aid. It should contain enough positives so that you enjoy rereading it. Beyond the description of what went well, the same spirit of inquiry can be brought to a positive issue as a negative issue. If something went well, how do you feel about it? What was your attitude of mind leading up to the positive outcome? Would there be value in repeating this experience in other contexts?

A quick way of reminding yourself to include positives and negatives is to draw a felt-tip pen face on completing each entry. The face can be a smiley face, or one with a downturned mouth, showing clearly whether you are criticising or congratulating yourself. Alternatively, you can conclude every journal entry with two questions: 'What did I do well?' and 'What did I not do so well?'

Exercise 1
Think of a routine task that you have to do at your clinic or workplace on a regular basis. This could be keeping up with your paperwork, ordering new stock, advertising or writing to colleagues. Find three strengths and three weaknesses that you have in relation to this task. Notice whether you deliberately chose a task at which you are successful or one in which you have difficulties. Your choice would influence whether it was easier to identify your strengths or weaknesses. Reflect on what you have noticed about the way you view yourself.

Exercise 2
Remember an important test or exam you had to take, such as your driving test, a music exam or your professional

qualification. Think back to the preparation for the exam. What did you do well, and what did you not do so well? Reflect on whether you have repeated this pattern or whether it only happened once.

Exercise 3

Think of an incident that happened at work with a client or colleague. Write about it honestly and factually, including both your thoughts and your emotions. When you have finished the description, ask yourself four questions:

- What was good about the situation?

- What was bad about the situation?

- What were my strengths?

- What were my weaknesses?

Use these questions to trigger self-reflection, and finish with an action plan.

JOURNAL EXAMPLE

A woman booked a nutritional appointment for her five-year-old son, who had hyperactivity and food allergies. When she asked if it was all right to bring her three-year-old daughter as well, I explained that I wanted to focus on the patient and it would be better if she could find alternative arrangements for her daughter.

However, all three of them came to the appointment, together with a baby in a car seat. My heart sank, wondering how this crowd would fit into my clinic room, and more importantly how I would get the information I needed if the mother's attention was taken up with three children. I got out my box of toy cars and a basket of dinosaurs and play people. The little boy (I will call him Tom) was delighted with the box of cars, tipping them onto the floor from a great height so that they fell with a crash and woke up the baby. The mother picked up the crying baby, and the little girl who had been happily looking around the room suddenly became needy and wanted to sit on her mother's knee. The mother tried to persuade her to look at the toys but, when the girl picked up a car, Tom was furious and chased her away.

Ten or 15 minutes passed in this manner before we could start the consultation. Tom was aggressive towards his sister and soon got bored with the toys, wanting to escape the clinic room and explore the rest of the building. Luckily the door handle was too high up for him to reach, but he spent several minutes jumping for it and kicking the door.

Eventually the mother settled the baby, found a favourite toy in her bag for the little girl and was free to tell me about Tom's weekly diet. The consultation was a hasty, scrambled affair that took half the time I had planned for it, because the taxi arrived early to take them home. Packing up to leave, the mother realised she had forgotten her chequebook and promised to post my fee to me.

WHAT WAS GOOD ABOUT THE SITUATION?

I had a vivid demonstration of Tom's hyperactivity, which told me far more than a question-and-answer session would have done. It was also good that the door handle was high up!

WHAT WAS BAD ABOUT THE SITUATION?

I had to do a lot of clearing up after they had gone, throwing away a couple of toy cars that Tom had broken and picking up pieces of tissue that he had shredded. I am unsure whether I will get paid. This mother has good intentions but she has her hands full and I'm not sure if she will remember to post a cheque.

WHAT WERE MY STRENGTHS?

I am pleased that I had guessed that this might happen, and I provided plenty of toys. This has happened to me once before so I could remain outwardly calm. My main strength is in my case taking. When I look through my notes, I can see that I have got all the information I need, even though it felt rushed and it was often interrupted.

WHAT WERE MY WEAKNESSES?

Because this has happened before, I think I might have a boundary issue here. I need to make it clear that for the first appointment the mother should just bring the child who is to be the patient. For a hyperactive child like Tom, it should be every appointment without siblings, and yet, having just gone through a chaotic consultation, I still did not make this clear when we were booking the next appointment. I took it for granted that the mother would realise it's difficult for me to work with so many children in the room making so much noise. But she lives like that all the time, so I guess she took it for granted that I could cope.

THINGS I NEED TO DO

- If the mother sends a cheque within a week, I will phone her to thank her, and stress that the next appointment should be for Tom by himself.

- If the mother does not send a cheque by next week, I will send a bill with a reminder that the next appointment should be with Tom by himself.

- Be more definite with parents that my consulting room is too small for any more than one child.

Letter to yourself

Writing a letter to yourself can help clarify your thoughts, feelings or action plans. It is most effective if it is written in an affectionate manner, starting with 'Dear my name' and voiced as if you were speaking directly to yourself. For some people, writing to themselves in a loving way can be very healing, especially if they are normally self-critical.

The letter can be written from the positive aspects of the Adult, Parent or Child in the manner of transactional analysis (see Chapter 1). Your own inner nurturing Parent can write to you congratulating you on your success, reassuring you about your failings or giving advice about an action plan. Your inner Adult can write in a way that is quietly contemplative and reflective. Your inner free Child can write to you in a playful, intuitive way.

Writing a letter to yourself can be a comfort in times of conflict, trauma or illness, especially if it is done through the gentle voice of the caring Parent. The Child's voice is more excitable, vibrant and playful. It demands to be heard and is particularly useful during times of stagnation and boredom.

Exercise 1

Start with a simple statement of 'I'm no good at…' This could be your inner critic telling you that you are no good with computers ('I'm a technophobe'), or no good with children or animals, or you have no luck with gardening or DIY ('I couldn't put up a shelf'), or you cannot cook or ride a bicycle. For most people, there will be a skills deficiency that has become a stuck point so that they refuse to retrain or reconsider. The general feeling about the skills deficiency is one of negativity, sometimes covered up by self-depreciation.

Now write a letter to yourself from your kindly, reassuring, protective inner Parent in answer to this statement. Be encouraging and helpful, and remind your negative self of other successes with parallel circumstances. You might want to take this letter as far as an action plan to initiate change, but you don't have to. The first step is compassion and reassurance. When you have finished this letter, sign it with love and take the time to reread it and absorb what you have written. Then do a short self-reflection on what it feels like.

Exercise 2

Remember a time when you were involved in a very intense period of work lasting several weeks. Perhaps you were working to a deadline when you had to do a presentation or take an exam, or perhaps it was just the season when your work intensifies every year.

Write a letter to yourself from your vibrant, excitable, playful and loving inner Child. Give yourself emotional support – imagine the child on your knee, giving you cuddles – and suggest ideas about what you can do together to have fun when the work eases off. Listen to your inner Child telling you that hard work is always followed by playtime. When you have finished the letter, sign it with love and affection. Leave it for a day or two and then reread it and do a short reflection on what it feels like.

Exercise 3

Think of an uncomfortable relationship that you have currently or have had in the past with a client or colleague at work. This was someone who pushed your buttons, didn't appreciate you, challenged you or upset you. Write a letter to yourself from your calm inner Adult or your compassionate inner Parent. Allow that letter to be full of reassurance and praise, focusing on the things that went well even if these were few and far between.

JOURNAL EXAMPLE

My dear Marianne,

I'm delighted to have this opportunity to write to you and say how much I appreciated watching you teach at the acupuncture college this year.

I want you to stop worrying about your problematic student. You know who I mean. He was clearly carrying issues from his own past, and, although his challenges were very uncomfortable for you, you managed to remain outwardly calm and ethical with him. Well done! His accusations of racism were unfounded, and, when you pointed out that at least 80 per cent of the class were international students, he grinned in an almost guilty way and dropped the subject. I want you to remember that you have always really enjoyed the multicultural diversity of your class.

He was deeply angry and wanted to challenge and irritate you so that he could feel the satisfaction of power over you. After all he is very young! It was very tough for you, but you learned a lot and I am proud of you. You learned to manage his interruptions, asking him to talk to you later, or asking the rest of the class to give him feedback. You started thinking differently when you were preparing the lesson plans and I'm sure that the whole class benefited from your careful listing of objectives at the beginning of each lesson and your plenaries at the end.

You had some high achievers who were a real joy to work with, and some middle-rankers who pulled up their grades with your help and guidance. But what I'd really like you to remember from this year is the last day, when you got everyone to appreciate and thank each other for working together, and many of them turned to thank you as well. Even your angry rebel mumbled thanks and – mark this! – held eye contact with you.

I know that your inner judge wants to pick up on all the minor things that you did not do well, but tell it to go to sleep. You have done extremely well and learned a lot.

From your loving self,
Marianne

Subjective–objective

It is sometimes said that everyone sees slight variations on colours, and when they talk about red, blue or yellow they are actually talking about their interpretation of the colour rather than impartial reality. In the same way, it is often difficult for someone to describe an event or situation from a neutral viewpoint, when the tendency is to view it through their own eyes. Everyone is the central character or starring role of their own life history; and yet, if they want to fully understand what has happened, they will need a wider horizon or bird's eye view of events to be objective.

One way to do this is to divide the event into a factual description and an emotional description. The factual description needs to be very cool and unbiased, as if written by a top-quality historian or a policeman presenting evidence in court. The description should be given in a logical order. The sentence structure should be in the form of 'this happened', or 'this person said'. The language needs to avoid emotive adjectives. These are the descriptive words that give emotional impact, such as kind, irritable, good, spiteful, attractive and so on.

Once the factual description has been completed, the event is then written about again from an emotional perspective, which should be highly personal and focusing on feelings and emotions. The language in this description can contain as many emotive adjectives as you please, and it should be written from the personal point of view, such as 'I felt'.

When you have completed both these descriptions, leave them for an hour or two before you reread them, and then write a short self-reflection on what you have noticed.

Exercise 1

Write two short descriptions about what you had for breakfast this morning and whether you had this meal alone or with someone. The first description should be objective and factual, and the second one should be subjective and emotional. Remember to differentiate between 'a bowl of cornflakes with milk and half a cup of coffee' (factual) and 'a delicious bowl of my favourite cereal and my necessary half cup of reviving strong coffee' (emotional).

Exercise 2

Choose an article from your local newspaper, and read through it carefully. Analyse whether it is emotional or factual. Is the writer being objective, or trying to influence your opinion through emotional storytelling? Go through the article a second time and circle any words or phrases that appear to you to be non-factual.

Exercise 3

Remember an incident at work with your clients or colleagues that had an emotional impact on you. Perhaps you felt angry, sad, frustrated, jealous or embarrassed, for example. Write about it in your journal, first in a cool, logical and factual way, and then in an emotional way. Finally do some self-reflection on what you have discovered.

JOURNAL EXAMPLE

FACTUAL DESCRIPTION

A new patient phoned up, asking to make an appointment. The homeopath gave the usual details of appointment times and fees, and arranged to send further information to the patient. She fleetingly noticed that the patient had a strong and confident voice.

When the patient arrived for the appointment, the homeopath was struck by her tall, upright deportment and her clear, confident voice. The consultation proceeded as normal, with the homeopath encouraging the patient to express herself freely during the hour and a half appointment. The woman revealed that she was an actress, and the homeopath replied that she did not watch TV but she was interested to know if her patient was typecast. The woman reflected on this, and mentioned several films that she had been in, each with a different character. The last of these films was one that the homeopath had seen, and for the first time she realised who her patient was.

EMOTIONAL DESCRIPTION

Oh, I feel such a fool. My patient was AD! She is an extremely famous actress that even I have heard of and admire. She booked in using her married name, not her stage name, and I totally failed to recognise her voice or her face, but just treated her as Jo Public. I thought it was odd that she had such a big voice on the phone, but it didn't dawn on me to think further. When she finally mentioned a film that I had heard of, a sort of shock went through me, and I spoke without thinking, 'Oh, you're her!' She just smiled at me, and I smiled back like a fool. Then I realised what I was doing and looked at my notes, to try to pull myself together and catch up with what I had been asking her. It took several minutes before I could fully engage with her again, and focus on her as an interesting case rather than gazing at her like an awestruck fan.

REFLECTIONS

I notice that I have used the word 'fool' a couple of times in my emotional description, and that describes my sense of embarrassment and lack...lack of what? Lack of common knowledge, lack of wit and lack of social manners. I began the consultation as a professional, and I think I did well, but the sudden, late recognition of my patient threw me completely and made me behave like a silly teenager. My inner judge is very critical of this.

I wonder how my patient felt in being treated like Jo Public? I'm now beginning to think that it must have been a refreshing experience for her to go to a practitioner where she could talk from the depths of her being without her stage persona getting in the way. It must have felt as if she was being appreciated for who she really was. And on my side, it was much better that I didn't recognise her at first, because I was able to be my professional self.

The moment of realisation was embarrassing, but from the way she smiled I think she saw the funny side of it. Although the moment felt as if it was stretching into hours, it didn't really take long until I was back into the case again. Learning about the films that she had been in, and her feelings about them, helped me understand her very well. I feel I have made a very good prescription for her.

The positive achievement journal

One thing that I have noticed from working for many years with adult students is that many can have a major lack of confidence in both new material they are learning and in their own innate abilities. A lot of this comes from the adult learner's perception that, because they are grown up, they 'ought' to know everything and must be lacking if they have to return to studying. Children are far more accepting of the learning experience but for some adults it can feel strange and uncomfortable. This is amplified if the teaching methodology puts the adult learners into what I affectionately call 'the baby bird syndrome', expecting them to open their beaks and swallow the teaching whole. Adult learners do much better if they can self-direct a portion of their learning, calling upon their previous knowledge, understanding, experience, ability or skills.

If adult learners are expected to engage with self-reflection, this can open up more areas in which they feel anxiety. Confidence can be lacking in topics that were taught badly in the first place, or attitudes that were inherited from parents and carers.

I recommend that anyone who is lacking in confidence tries out either writing a boasting list or writing a positive achievement journal. The boasting list is written once and includes anything that you were born with, you achieved or you received; the positive achievement journal is written daily and should only include things that you initiate.

THE BOASTING LIST

This should focus on your strengths and not mention any weaknesses at all. I have observed that some lists start with a modest three to five points and then come to a halt, demonstrating how hard it is for some people to feel good about themselves. You need to include life skills, personal attributes, qualifications, specialised experience, commendations from other people and so on. The boasting list has no boundaries, and can include examples such as:

- a good sense of humour
- a previous career in customer relations
- experience with the elderly or children
- being good at listening
- good exam results when you were a teenager
- having a good telephone manner
- positive feedback from your last assessment
- praise from a friend or your grandmother.

THE POSITIVE ACHIEVEMENT JOURNAL

This can be written into its own self-contained notebook, or combined with the self-reflective journal. Whichever way you do it, try to put it in a format that is quick and easy to reread. Glancing through a week or two weeks' worth of achievements will certainly make you feel good. You should set a target of writing down between one and five positive achievements every day, however small. A positive achievement is anything that you initiated and makes you feel good. Unlike the boasting list, you cannot include things that other people did or said, because you did not initiate them. Examples of positive achievements are:

- getting to work on time
- remaining calm with an aggressive client
- remembering to pay a bill
- offering your seat on public transport to someone in more need
- phoning your mother
- completing your assignment on time
- returning a phone call to an anxious patient
- updating your website
- getting to bed early, so that you have a good rest
- going to the gym.

Usually the positive achievement journal is written about everything that happens throughout your day, but you can focus it on one topic if you're working towards a particular goal. For example, you could use it as part of your practitioner development plan, or a way of logging your studies. If there is anything you are particularly proud of, when you have gone above and beyond what is expected of you or what you expected of yourself, this should be highlighted in the positive achievement journal. You can go even further, and remind yourself of this extra achievement, by making it into a screensaver or printing it out and sticking it on the fridge.

Exercise 1
Starting a new page in your journal, write down five positive achievements for yesterday, four for the day before yesterday, three for the day before that, two for the day before that, and one for the day before that. Do not repeat the same achievement for each day, but aim for 15 different achievements covering the last five days. Do not write down anything negative. Reflect on what this felt like.

Exercise 2

This is a variation on the positive achievement journal, where it becomes task specific. Choose a task that appears overwhelming, stressful or simply boring, and one you find yourself resistant to doing. Decide where you're going to write your positive achievements, and make sure they are easily available to reread. Don't put them on scraps of paper that will get lost on the desk. Every day you have done something that has contributed towards your task, record it and congratulate yourself. You can only write positives. Do not allow yourself to write down any negatives or failures. When the task has come to its natural completion, reflect in your journal on what you have learned.

JOURNAL EXAMPLE

I have come to the end of my college training – I have graduated! – but the next hurdle is providing a professional development plan and portfolio for registration. I need to decide my plans for the next year. I don't know where to begin! My supervisor suggested that I set aside an hour or two each week to clarify my ideas and begin the portfolio. He said that I should record everything I do in a positive achievement journal.

WEEK 1

- Printed off the portfolio requirements and read through them, marking them with a highlighter pen.

- Phoned up my friend and asked what she was doing about her portfolio, to get some ideas.

WEEK 2

- Spent an hour looking at other people's websites! Scary at first but after a while I began to see what I could offer.

- Looked at the printing website that my friend recommended, to get ideas for colours and themes so I can match my website and business cards.

WEEK 3

- Wrote a short list of what I might put on my website.

- Decided I could borrow a camera and take some photos for my website – feel really excited about this!

- Drafted out a letter that I could send my clients, saying I have graduated and these are my new terms and conditions.

- Had another look at the printing website and made notes on what sort of impact I want to make when advertising.

WEEK 4

- Met with my supervisor again, and showed him the draft letter for my clients – it only needed a few adjustments, so I was very pleased!

- Printed the client letter and sent it off to everyone on my mailing list – had to organise my mailing list as well. Two tasks achieved in one go!

- Booked to go to a workshop for running a small business in March – surprised myself! It should be good and I'll meet other people.

- Ordered my business cards.

- Signed up to get the European newsletter – decided I will record in this journal every time I read the newsletter.

WEEK 5

- Started a draft of my professional development plan – I feel clearer about it now, because it includes my business plan, website, business cards, etc., as well as my ongoing study plans.

- Read a couple of reviews of new textbooks to decide if I want to study in that direction – surprised myself, because it felt a very grown-up thing to do!

- Looked on the internet for other small workshops, hoping to find one about internet marketing. Found a distance learning course – will that do? I will continue researching next week.

- Read my first copy of the European newsletter.

- Drafted out some text for my website and started to research into companies that build websites.

REFLECTIONS AFTER FIVE WEEKS

I feel great! Knowing that I will have to write something in my positive achievement journal has made me more proactive, and doing things in small steps has made it less overwhelming. I'm beginning to feel clear about my professional development plan and I'm getting more organised. I noticed that I wrote a couple of times that I surprised myself by being organised. Recording each action as if it was a big achievement feels very good. Yes, I like being nice to myself! Well done me.

CHAPTER 5

ADVANCED TOOLS AND TECHNIQUES

> Observing herself
> she plants the dry bulbs
> for next year

The self-reflective journal is a form of learning journal, in which the writer explores experience, observation or theory in order to enhance their personal or professional life. The mature reflective journal, when compared with that of the novice, will have less description and more consideration and investigation. Over time it becomes more objective, with careful and balanced inquiry from many different angles. Critical thinking and self-questioning are used to increase understanding. The viewpoint ceases to be so personal, but takes into account wider implications, such as the impact of other people and their perspectives; the writer's prior emotions or experiences; or historical or sociological considerations.

Moon (2006) writes about four levels of depth in reflection and includes in the fourth level: 'There is clear evidence of standing back from an event and there is mulling over and engagement' (p.162).

Some people set aside dedicated time and effort to improve their self reflection skills. They may research through the literature or work alongside a tutor or supervisor who recommends new techniques or theory. Research could also be done through questioning colleagues, although often politeness and respect regarding another's journal work prevents sharing.

Other people reach the deeper levels of mature reflection organically through rereading and reviewing what they have written. They may have an informal attitude to theory, picking it up or dropping it according to its relevance to their personal needs.

As their critical thinking develops, they consider their reflective skills and take note of what has been effective. They may intuitively change their reflective style so that their journal evolves to fulfil needs as they arise.

The following reflection is from one of the graduates of the distance learning course in which I am involved. She describes working with her emotions through the reflective journal, which would effectively discharge them although they would later resurface. Finally, she reached a point where she could allow her intuition to take over, which enabled her to let go of the old patterns. It's a good example of intuitive development, through the journal.

> I enjoy reading my old reflective journals, because I can see how I have improved. In earlier times, I used self-reflective journals mostly to perceive my emotions and thoughts clearly. It was fun to discover the way I had reacted towards this and that, and through this work I had a good experience in understanding myself better.
>
> Lately I realised that my self-reflection pattern had changed, in a more constructive way. For example, I did many self-reflections last year to support my sister who was suffering from anxiety attacks. I had to think clearly about my emotions so that I wouldn't react impulsively. There was lots of anger and sadness towards medicine. I tried to forgive myself for having these emotions, and cultivate compassion for my sister. From doing that I could avoid being reactive in front of her and consequently end up burned out. But those emotions were still there in me.
>
> One day I felt there was something new occurring within me; I didn't know what it was. So I went to my desk and took my pen to start self-reflecting, and found out what it was: 'It was no use having those negative emotions as they wouldn't improve the situation.' I had never had this kind of thought before. Then next moment I found myself coming from a more practical point of view, as opposed to a sentimental point of view. From then I could let go of those emotional thoughts easily, and not in a manner of sacrifice. Consequently I felt more relaxed about helping her out, and, interestingly enough, things got much better.

From keeping journals I found that I could see the various phases that I went through, which was extremely helpful in my personal development. (personal communication, previously unpublished)

The uses of self-reflection

In the previous chapter I started with a tentative list of the uses of self-reflection at novice level. As the journal writer becomes more familiar with writing regularly, they may start to expand beyond working with observations, thoughts and feelings to a wider horizon. The topics that are investigated within the journal start to have broader personal, professional, social and organisational implications. My tentative list of the uses of self-reflection has doubled, and no doubt other items could be added as well:

- Review aspects of your work, and assess your strengths and weaknesses to initiate change.

- Explore a specific incident in order to understand it at a deeper level.

- Learn from your experiences in order to provide a better service for others.

- Develop self-questioning and critical thinking to gain a wider viewpoint.

- Observe your emotions and make links to other emotional responses you have had.

- Explore the past and present in order to make action plans for the future.

- Build up your self-confidence.

- Review an issue through other people's eyes to open up multiple viewpoints.

- Expose your attitudes, prejudices and beliefs and decide if they are still relevant.

- Appreciate the complexity of most situations and take ownership of your part in them.

- Assess any legal, political, social and organisational implications.

- Engage in ethical and moral dilemmas to clarify your position and action plan.

- Clarify observations and relate this to theory.

Transformation through self-reflection

As I wrote in the previous chapter, the advantages of self-reflection are that you can deal with issues as they arise, investigating them and releasing their impact upon you. This empowers you and benefits those you come in contact with, such as patients, colleagues, clients, family and friends. It is a cleansing and refining process that can gradually remove many of your prejudices and fixed beliefs. It is an opportunity to refresh your thinking and reaffirm your values. You will become more self-aware and more objective. Your critical thinking will improve, and you will learn to acknowledge your emotions without being ruled by them. You will have an effective overview of different aspects of your work.

As the reflective journal becomes more mature, it can provide a forum for working with more complex dilemmas, where there is no straightforward answer. You can begin to view situations through other people's eyes, opening up new understandings. You can investigate your responsibility, and identify what is your business and what belongs to other people. You can clarify your boundaries and monitor how effective they are. You can use your journal to review your options and make necessary decisions. You can wrestle with moral and ethical dilemmas, although it is often advisable to go for a second opinion about these after working with the journal.

The more you use your journal, the more it contributes towards your mental, emotional and spiritual well-being. You might not necessarily write more for each journal entry, but as you mature you enter into it at a deeper level and you return to it more often as a welcome place of peace and privacy. Your self-knowledge increases and so does your understanding, tolerance and appreciation of your clients and colleagues. Any stress felt at work is more quickly diffused, and as a practitioner you are less likely to burn out.

As with all the methods and techniques in this book, I encourage you to experiment and play with my suggestions and add your own reflections. Feel free to engage with these techniques, and review, reformat, restructure or rewrite to suit yourself.

Dialogue with yourself

In contrast with recording conversation, dialoguing is an invented conversation between you and someone or something else. The technique of dialogue could be compared to role-play with another person acting out the part of your problem, or the Gestalt use of an empty chair to represent the other, allowing you to speak to them and hear their reply.

You can dialogue with anything at all. For example, it is an interesting and empowering experience to acknowledge that there are different aspects to your personality and, taking this further, allow them to have a voice. Using the journal, you can create a conversation that allows each aspect to express itself. This could be your logical, responsible side having a discussion with your artistic, creative side. It could be your inner Child arguing with your inner Parent. It could be the rebellious teenager that you were, talking to the conscientious adult that you have become. Or vice versa.

You can write a dialogue in your journal between yourself and a colleague, client, friend or family member, allowing your knowledge and intuition to provide the other person's words. You can do this in order to prepare what you will say to them, in the manner of role-play. You can dialogue to try to understand the other person and your relationship with them. You can do it in order to investigate your own attitudes, fears, wishes and demands from them.

You can even use this method to explore your relationship with an object, a season, a festival, an event, the work you do, institutions, figures that appear in dreams, animals or relatives who have passed away.

These sorts of dialogues can enhance your understanding of complex situations, enabling you to come to terms with difficult issues in your life or your work. Inner conflict can feel very uncomfortable for someone who is torn between two directions in their life, such as a choice between 'want' and 'ought'. Writing a dialogue in the journal can give birth to an appreciation that both sides have their positive aspects, and it is possible simply to enjoy the contrast. From antagonism with self, the viewpoint can shift into spoilt for choice.

Exercise 1

In this exercise you are asked to write an imaginary conversation with an adult who had a positive influence on your childhood, such as a parent, teacher, music tutor or sports coach. Before you start writing, spend a few minutes remembering and visualising them. Include their appearance, their voice, their body language, and what they taught you. Begin your dialogue with thanking them for being the role model that they were, and your reasons for having chosen them as an influence on your childhood. Allow their side of the conversation to come to you intuitively, and don't question any of their statements that surprise you. Just go with the flow and see what evolves.

Exercise 2

Write a dialogue with one of the machines that you use a lot in your life – for example, your personal computer, your washing machine, your music player, your TV or your car. Choose a machine that occasionally goes wrong despite complex electronic engineering and a high price tag. Express all your frustration with the unreliability of this machine, and once again allow your intuition to provide its voice, attitude and answers.

Exercise 3

Another use of the dialogue technique is as a rehearsal, when you anticipate a difficult conversation with someone. You can imagine the dialogue in advance in order to do a dry run. Using the reflective journal to prepare for the dialogue is positive action rather than just worrying.

Sit quietly for a few minutes before you begin, breathing deeply and relaxing your muscles. Allow the person you are going to dialogue with come to your mind and remember how they would sit, if they were in your chair right now. What would their body language be? Try sitting like they do.

This allows you to begin the dialogue with them in a more grounded, unprejudiced way. Then turn to your journal, and write out a dialogue with them, allowing their answers to arise spontaneously in your mind.

Exercise 4

Choose a situation where you have a dilemma, and cannot decide whether to take one pathway or another. Set up a dialogue between the two sides of your character that want to go in different directions, and see where the discussion takes you.

After doing any of these exercises, write a short reflection in your journal about your experience of doing it, and any insights you have had.

JOURNAL EXAMPLE

Mature me: I've been working here at the adult education centre for 15 years, writing and running my Health at Home courses. Now the adult education centre is offering us teacher training.

Youthful me: Why would I want to have teacher training? I have 15 years of experience! I always get good feedback from the students at the end of term, and when someone observes my lessons from the principal's office, they are pleased with my work.

Mature me: Everyone benefits if I do my teacher training. My students get a better teacher, the education centre raises its reputation and I gain new skills.

Youthful me: It's doubtful how many new skills I will gain. There will be a lot of time spent reading books and writing essays. It will be boring.

Mature me: I will get the opportunity to share ideas with other teachers, and to observe other teachers' lessons.

Youthful me: I am a teacher already! I shouldn't have to go back and sit in a classroom again.

Mature me: Why so resistant? You usually say that learning is exciting.

Youthful me: I just hate it when there is a pedantic teacher at the front of the class, telling you what you ought to think.

Mature me: Where does that come from?

Youthful me: My experiences at university, I suppose. I hated it.

Mature me: Why do you think teacher training would be like that? Surely they will be teaching lots of exciting new methodologies?

Youthful me: Well, I suppose so.

Mature me: What else? Why do you think I shouldn't do teacher training?

Youthful me: It might turn out that I'm a fraud – that I'm not a good teacher after all.

Mature me: That could be very embarrassing. But it's not so likely, is it? I always get good feedback from the students.

Youthful me: We have fun in the lessons, and my students have a good time. But that's not the same as presenting the material in the best possible way.

Mature me: Perhaps you're right – perhaps it would be a mistake to go to teacher training.

Youthful me: I would risk being shown up in front of the other teachers.

Mature me: It's not as if I would need my teaching certificate for anything else. I'm not going to start teaching in schools or colleges.

Youthful me: Hang on a moment! That's limiting my future, isn't it?

Mature me: It's the safer option. I could do the teacher training, but it looks like it will either tell me what I already know – or it will expose me to embarrassment because it will show me what I should have known about teaching all this time. In other words, it will either be boring or it will dent my self-esteem.

Youthful me: But where is my spirit of adventure? If I can bring fun into the lessons when I am a teacher, then surely I can bring fun into the lessons when I am a student?

Mature me: You mean we might enjoy it more, if I let you join in during the lessons?

Youthful me: That's it! I might be anxious about it but my positive side is my sense of fun and adventure.

Mature me: And I can do the research for the assignments, and be rewarded with the certificate.

REFLECTIONS

It was really helpful to identify that a lot of my resistance to further training came from fear. What I hadn't expected was the turnaround from the youthful me resisting training to the mature me resisting training and the youthful me wanting to go for it. It certainly sounds a more exciting venture now that I have done this exercise!

Reviewing a conversation

Relationships with people at work or at home can be complex, and at different times everyone has probably experienced dissatisfaction at the end of a conversation, wishing that they had expressed themselves differently. If the situation is very intense, you might find yourself rewriting your inner script many times over the next 24 hours, wishing that you had used a full range of eloquent words to make the other person truly understand you. Sadly, you cannot rewrite history, and the other person will never fully understand you because they cannot see the world through your eyes. But what you can do is understand yourself, which will enable you to let go of the conversation and feel more relaxed about the whole situation.

It is best not to review a conversation, consultation or interview when you're still in the heat of your emotional reaction. You will be unable to do it without bias, and you will almost always reach a conclusion that you were right and the other person was wrong. The mind does not like to be shown up as wrong, and will tend to justify itself. Allow a few hours or days to pass, until you are cooler and prepared to investigate what happened without prejudice.

Turn your page sideways, so that you have a landscape presentation, and divide the page into three columns. In the first column, write the conversation as accurately as possible, using a fresh line for each new comment. Try to be as honest as possible without rewriting history or adding any improvements to your side of the conversation. You don't need to include descriptive elements, such as where you were sitting or the time of day. Just focus on the words that were said. Email discussions are ideal for this kind of reflection, because you can cut and paste the conversation.

In the second column, write your feelings about what was going on, alongside each part of the conversation. These can include current feelings, as well as feelings you had at the time. In the final column, write your reflections, such as your observations, evaluations and conclusions.

You might feel the main difficulty with this exercise is remembering the conversation. Our ancestors from one or two centuries ago were trained to memorise long conversations, so be reassured that your brain is capable of it. In this century, we rely on modern technology to access information easily, so memory training has become less important. I recommend that you get into the habit of writing down key words immediately after interesting conversations, whether you intend to do a review or not. These will act as triggers to remember the rest of the conversation.

An abbreviated version of reviewing the conversation can be done several days or a week after it happened, using a brief description of the conversation in the first column. In this case the conversation won't be accurately written, but just given as an outline. The other two columns are done as before, describing your feelings in relation to the conversation, and then reflecting on this.

Exercise 1
Write down a conversation that you had, as soon as possible after the event. Do not be tempted to rewrite history or present your own words in a new and improved version. Leave this for a day or two and then divide your page into three columns, labelling them 'facts', 'feelings' and 'reflections'. Put the conversation into the facts column. Working slowly, think carefully about what you want to put in the other two columns.

Don't worry if the columns don't tally; you can still learn from this.

Exercise 2

Go to your email inbox, and find a short dialogue that you had with a work colleague. It does not need to be anything controversial but it needs to be something in which you had a conversation and there was more than one point of view. Divide your page into three columns and copy and paste the email dialogue into your first column. Label the other two columns 'feelings' and 'reflections' and add comments. When you have finished, reflect further on what you have discovered.

Figure 5.1 is a journal example taken from an email, showing the conversation, feelings and reflections.

JOURNAL EXAMPLE

Email conversation	Feelings	Reflections
Me: I heard that you were trying to email me, and I tried to email you in return, but it seems as if our emails are not arriving. Please let me know if you receive this one.		I was too casual about this, when my colleague told me the student was trying to get in touch.
Student: I am happy to have your email and I am sorry for this happening between us. I have been trying to get in touch with you for the last month. I thought you must be on holiday. I wonder how I can contact you in future if our email system is still having a problem?	I was really shocked to discover she has been trying to get in touch with me for the last month. I am her personal tutor and she should be able to get support from me. My colleague had to remind me twice to follow up on this student. I feel guilty and cross with myself.	I should have kept a record of when I sent emails to her, so that it did not run on for a month.

Me: I have not been on holiday. I read emails nearly every day and try to reply the same day. If you send an email and I do not reply promptly, please send a message to any of the other staff asking them to contact me.	I was trying to self-justify and cover my tracks. I almost blamed her for not trying hard enough or not writing to the other staff. Do I really reply to emails so promptly?	I have written to the staff to explain that I might have to involve them. This has been a wake-up call for me, and I will do an audit on how promptly I do read and answer emails.
Student: Thank you very much. I will keep in touch with you.		Email failure is one of the drawbacks of internet learning, but luckily it does not happen very often. I will put a message out to all students, telling them what to do if this happens to them.

Figure 5.1 Review of an email conversation with feelings and reflections

Fork in the road

Sometimes during times of quiet reflection about an issue such as a conversation, a relationship or a decision, there is a realisation that the outcome could have gone in any direction. A fork in the road had been reached, and for a moment nobody knew which would be the chosen path. Afterwards, there can be a sense of regret wondering if the wrong choice had been made, or curiosity about the lost options.

It is an interesting experience to use your imagination to play out what might have happened if another direction had been taken after all. To do this, you can ask yourself the question, 'What if…?' Working from your knowledge of the other people or the situation, together with your imagination, write the scenario or screenplay describing what would have happened if another choice had been taken. You can have fun wildly fantasising, but you will learn far more if you keep it as realistic as possible. As you work through the options, you might find that there are more and more choices available. Each time, ask the question again, 'What if...?'

This technique has been used in various stories, books, movies and TV films, showing the two different stories each playing out to fulfil their destiny in parallel universes. Some authors or directors have come to the conclusion that the outcome would be the same or similar whichever decision was made, in the manner of 'all roads lead to Rome'. You might come to the same conclusion, or you might decide the outcome would have been completely different.

Exercise 1

Remember an expensive purchase that you had to make within the past year or two. It could be an item of furniture for your office, a machine such as a new computer, a vehicle or signing up for further training. With any of these you would have carefully deliberated, weighing up cost, value for money, suitability and so on. Take yourself back to the moment of irresolution, and ask yourself, 'What if I had chosen the other option?' Using your imagination, write up the story of what would have happened with the alternative choice, until you reach the next turning point, and ask again, 'What if...?' Reflect on what you discover.

Exercise 2

Remember the last time a patient cancelled at the last minute or failed to turn up. Take a few minutes to remember or imagine the impact this had on your schedule and play with it a little, offering yourself alternatives and asking, 'What if?' Reflect on what you discover.

For example, you can ask yourself:

- What if you remember this patient has done this several times before?

- What if you phone this patient to find out why they haven't come and they tell you firmly that the appointment is for next week?

- What if you phone this patient, and they offer to drop everything and come immediately?

- What if you have a lot of paperwork to do and appreciate the extra free time?

- What if...?

Exercise 3

Think of a situation where you were under a lot of pressure, and had to make quick decisions. It doesn't matter if your decisions were good ones at the time or not. In order to review the situation, write about what happened in your journal, and ask yourself 'what if' you had taken one or many different alternatives. Would the outcome have been the same or different?

JOURNAL EXAMPLE

A new patient came to see me yesterday. She was in her early 40s and had come about irregular and prolonged periods. She was dressed in quiet but fashionable dark colours with expensive jewellery. Her face was, to me, quite striking because of the deep lines from nose to mouth, making her look unbearably sad. This was echoed by the sadness in her eyes, and I prepared myself to hear a history of grief or depression.

She was willing to talk, but did not talk easily, as if it was a rare occurrence for her to have the opportunity to talk about herself. It gradually came out that she was married to a politician who worked internationally. When he was at home, he was busy with meetings or working at his computer. She used to work part-time for him but was now working as a personal assistant to a lawyer. She said she felt accustomed to coming home to an empty house and meals for one.

I asked if she had children and she said no, it hadn't worked out. She made it clear that this was a closed subject and she didn't want to talk about it. She talked briefly about her husband's social life when he was abroad and I got the fleeting impression that she was saying he had affairs when he was away; but I didn't feel it was appropriate to ask more about this. I gathered they didn't have much of a sex life due to her periods and his travelling.

The consultation was slow and heavy and I found myself talking to her very gently and compassionately. I got the feeling that she would clam up if I pushed her too far, and yet I was hard put to get the information I needed. Everything pointed towards a state of grief, and yet it was all in veiled language; and when I asked outright if she was depressed, she said no, not at all.

By the end of the consultation, I had just about enough information to make my first homeopathic prescription, and I booked her in for a follow-up. I hope that in the next appointment, when she is more comfortable talking to me, she will go deeper and talk more about how this lifestyle has an impact on her.

My first reflections were that I had to work hard during the session to be unthreatening and gentle with her. I felt there were a lot of subjects that were taboo. This was frustrating for me, because until I understand her character and her feelings I cannot make a really good prescription for her.

WHAT IF I HAD STOPPED THE CONSULTATION AND RE-CONTRACTED?

I could have explained to her that, in order to get a good prescription, I need to understand her moods and feelings as well as physical symptoms. I need to differentiate between 4000 remedies. I could have reassured her of confidentiality, and asked her to go deeper. Then in effect I could start again. In terms of the ego states, I had been in the role of gentle, reassuring Parent, encouraging her very defended Child. If I had stopped the consultation and re-contracted, this could have taken us out of these roles and allowed us to talk Adult to Adult. However, maybe she wasn't ready for this.

WHAT IF I HAD PRESSURISED HER TO OPEN UP AND TELL ME MORE?

I could have told her firmly that, unless she explained her case more clearly, I would not be able to help her. This represents a switch from nurturing Parent into critical

Parent, and brings up ethical dilemmas. On the one hand it could help me find a really good remedy for her, but on the other hand it might force her into abandoning homeopathy – or force her into unveiling stuff she is not ready to reveal.

WHAT IF SHE OPENED UP AND TOLD ME A LOT OF STUFF SHE HAS BEEN HOLDING ON TO FOR YEARS?

If I was right about the grief and sadness – and this is only my supposition – it has been carefully sealed into a box marked 'Do not open'. If she had opened it, it could have been traumatic for her. Would I have had the skill to hold her emotionally until she was in a safe space to go home? Would I have been left holding her trauma after she had gone? There are possible risks here.

WHAT IF I TAKE THIS CASE VERY SLOWLY, AND TELL HER THAT IT WILL TAKE SEVERAL MONTHS OF TREATMENT?

This is certainly kinder for her, allowing each remedy to work holistically, both on her hormones and her walled-off emotions. It would give her time to build up her confidence in me. I do believe that the periods will not be fully cured until the emotional state has been addressed. Will she agree to several months of treatment? Everyone wants a quick fix and her problem, as she sees it, is just physical. I have already told her that I work holistically but I don't think she fully understands the implications of this. She probably thinks I have not noticed any sadness.

WHAT IF I RECOMMEND FURTHER SUPPORT FOR HER?

If my prescriptions are effective, and I hope they are, then the lid may start to lift on her emotions. At that point I could recommend counselling, or, if she is still reluctant to talk, I could suggest healing. I have contacts in both fields whom I could recommend. Rather than my trying to support her on my own, it would be better if she was able to have additional support from other professionals.

REFLECTIONS

This has been helpful. I did the right thing in being very gentle with her. As a politician's wife, she's in a difficult position and needs to be reassured about confidentiality. As a patient holding on to possible trauma, she needs time to build up trust in me. I appreciate the need to take things slowly and not traumatise her further. I can tell her that her case is deep-seated and will take several appointments. I have two back-up plans for additional support for her. I will explain to her again how homeopathy works holistically on all levels.

Different points of view

Everyone looks at the world from their own point of view. If your internal compass points north, you might assume that it's the same for everyone else, but actually there are many other points to the compass. Looking at an experience or critical incident from other points of view can be a useful exercise because it moves you away from self-justification to a broader awareness of complexity. You will be able to take responsibility for your part in the story.

I remember with great affection doing a long and muddy walk along a disused railway track. I entered the town tired but triumphant, and started to cut across the main road. A woman rushed up to me and took me by the elbow, saying repeatedly, 'You're in the middle of the road – you should have crossed at the crossing!' She was extremely anxious and held onto me tightly, and I began to feel irritated. It took me several minutes to realise that with my sunglasses and silver trekking pole, she had assumed I was blind.

Begin your journal entry by writing your own view of the situation, describing what you experienced and what you perceived. Then rewrite the situation from the viewpoint of one of the other protagonists, looking at the world through their eyes, using their words and imagining their feelings. If you feel negativity or antipathy towards one of the other people, try to put this behind you and work in a way that is as unprejudiced as possible. Your negative feelings are signalling a lack of understanding towards that person, and this exercise will be extremely useful and insightful.

When you have written the points of view of as many of the other players as you wish, reflect on what you have learned, and ask yourself if there is anything that you would have done differently, and, if so, how you would act in the future.

Exercise 1

Imagine you are a CAM practitioner and a couple come to see you because their baby has an ongoing health condition. Added to this, one of them believes strongly in your therapy, while the other one prefers traditional, orthodox medicine. You can feel negativity and suspicion coming from this partner, and you try to be extra calm and professional, explaining as much as you can as you go along. After they have left, you become aware of how stressed you were during the consultation. Taking your journal, write about the experience in a neutral way to start with and then from your point of view, followed by the viewpoint of each of the other adults.

Exercise 2

Remember or imagine an occasion where you were asked to do a specific piece of work with a colleague. The instructions were not clear, and as it turned out you both had a different understanding of what was expected from you. Write about this first from your own perspective, and then from your colleague's point of view. Reflect on what you have learned.

Exercise 3

Choose a situation where you were with a client, friend or colleague and something they said or did rang a discordant note for you. Since then you have been puzzling to try to understand what was going on at the time. Write about this in your journal, first as an objective, factual description, and then about the different people's points of view. Afterwards, jot down some reflections about what you have learned.

JOURNAL EXAMPLE

A woman of 65 came to see me for a consultation. She had a serious disease and was receiving treatment from the hospital. The medication gave her severe side-effects, and she wanted to find out whether homeopathy could provide relief from these. I reassured her that the homeopathy would not interfere with the hospital medication in any way, and would most probably help with the side-effects. However, I emphasised the need for open communication with her consultant, and she agreed to inform him.

The homeopathic remedies did alleviate the side-effects and give her more energy. She continued to visit me over the course of two years during which time her disease stabilised. She had a very positive attitude, a deep religious faith, and she would talk to me very openly. I felt her love of life and I enjoyed the consultations.

Quite abruptly, she became worse again, and had to go into hospital for an operation. The next time I saw her, she appeared to have aged considerably, and walked with a stick and the help of her daughter. The daughter was neither as open nor as cheerful as her mother, but she watched me seriously as I questioned her mother to get the information I needed to prescribe. As they were leaving, the mother mentioned that her daughter was a lawyer. I saw both of them for several more appointments, and the daughter continued to be reserved and watchful.

My patient went into hospital again and the daughter phoned me up. She said she had doubts about homeopathy herself, but she could see it did no harm and her mother believed in it explicitly. Therefore, the daughter asked if I could help with remedies while her mother was recovering in hospital. On her return home, the daughter rang me again and asked me to make further prescriptions. I offered a home visit, but she said this wasn't an option – the community nurse would be calling and her mum would be tired. The daughter gave me some further information from her observations and we arranged for a phone consultation.

MY VIEWPOINT

My patient was a very interesting woman and I enjoyed the consultations very much. Both she and I knew the seriousness of her disease, and we both agreed that I was enhancing her quality of life rather than curing her. I found it more difficult to get on with her daughter, who sat in on the interviews but remained serious and thoughtful. I felt she was judging me, and it was a little bit unnerving to discover she was a lawyer. I was pleased when she asked for my help when her mother was in hospital.

My relationship with the mother was good so I was surprised when the daughter wouldn't let me do a home visit. I wondered if it was because she didn't want her mother to get overtired or because of the daughter's own issues. I chose to trust that she was being empathetic towards her mother rather than controlling; and I kept careful notes of all that happened.

THE DAUGHTER'S VIEWPOINT

I don't know why my mother chose to go to a homeopath, when the consultant could have given her something to deal with the side-effects of the first medication. The consultant must have been used to this. I don't believe in homeopathy and I was very suspicious at first, but I was quite surprised at how warm and friendly the consultation was. There was clearly an excellent rapport between my mother and the homeopath and that was valuable. Even if it was only placebo she was being given, I could see that it was helping her.

After the second operation, the consultant told me that there was not much hope and Mum would probably fade away. I decided to take time off work, move in with Mum and support her in every way possible. I knew that she would like to talk to her homeopath on the phone, and it would give her a boost. I also knew that there were some symptoms she would not mention directly to the homeopath, especially if she was tired. I had seen the level of information the homeopath needed to prescribe, so I decided to share what I had observed and let Mum have a friendly phone call.

THE MOTHER'S VIEWPOINT

The doctors at the hospital don't talk about it, and my daughter avoids it, but I know that I am dying. You don't get a disease like this without knowing. Last year my homeopath asked me a lot about my faith and it was a great relief to talk to someone about my spiritual beliefs. I really felt that she had time to listen to me, and she understood me. Her remedies helped with the side-effects, and at first I had a lot more energy. I have also felt calmer since seeing her, making it easier to face dying, and I'm sure this was from the remedies. I felt I could trust her.

REFLECTIONS

It was very helpful writing from the daughter's point of view, because I began to appreciate the deep love she had for her mother. When I spoke to her, she was quite reserved and appeared almost unemotional. Even though she was sceptical about homeopathy, she decided to give it the best possible chance by making sure I had enough information. I felt really moved while writing the mother's point of view. Talking about her spiritual beliefs had helped me find a prescription that would help her, but beyond this I had been able to relate to much of what she had said, so it touched me spiritually. Doing this exercise helped me see how rare such an opportunity must have been for her and its value for me.

Past, present and future

When an event, experience or incident is happening, it happens in the now and feels physically and emotionally relevant to the current time. But as reflection takes place, it is possible to see lots of strands and links to past thoughts and emotions. Experiences are not isolated, after all, but just a moment in time that is part of the continuum of your life journey. Everything that you are experiencing in the present can be informed by your past, and can contribute to your future experiences. This is excellent news if your current experiences are positive and uplifting, but if they are not then it is worth taking the time to explore and disconnect from past influences that are no longer relevant.

An interesting example is your attitude to money. When running workshops, I sometimes ask everyone to reflect upon their family's attitude towards money, and we make a long list of money-oriented statements, such as the following.

- 'Money doesn't grow on trees.'

- 'You shouldn't talk about money.'

- 'We can't afford expensive holidays.'

- 'Never borrow money.'

- 'The best things in life are free.'

These money statements can feel very powerful, like a truism or a proverb. It is only when we put them all together on the whiteboard that participants can start to laugh at them. Most probably you overheard similar statements when you were a small child up to the age of seven. At this age you did not have the ability to filter the information from your parents, and you believed everything absolutely. Information from your childhood becomes locked in place, and influences your behaviour for the rest of your life. Some of this is useful information such as fire burns and, if you walk in the road without looking, you could be hit by a vehicle; but other information from that time might not be relevant any longer.

The past can influence your current perceptions, beliefs and prejudices. If you have reacted to something in a particularly strong or uncharacteristic way, it might be because you're subconsciously linking it to some previous memories, some of which might go back to childhood. You can investigate it by self-questioning, using cues such as the following.

- Who does the person remind me of?

- When I was thinking that, whose voice was in my head?

- When has something similar happened before?

- When have I felt like this before?

- What was my judgement, and who has made that judgement of me in the past?

Experiment with trying some of the exercises that follow. As usual, if reading through these triggers an even better idea, then try that out in your journal.

Exercise 1

Consider your attitudes and opinions about food and exercise. It is likely that some of these were taken from your parents and carers at a young age, and some were developed through the influence of your peers before the age of 20. Begin with writing a long and personal list about your thoughts and feelings around food and exercise. Ask yourself reflective questions to see if you can identify where some or all of these opinions came from. For example:

- What are my opinions about food and exercise?

- What did my parents say about food or exercise?

- What did my siblings say?

- What did I observe my family doing with regards to food and exercise?

- When I was told off as a child about food, what was the message?

- What did my childhood friends say, and does this fit with what I observed?

- What did they teach us at school about these things?

- What did my teenage friends say about food or exercise?

- When I'm eating on my own, what emotions do I associate with it?

- When did I first feel like that about food?

Exercise 2

If you come across beliefs and attitudes that are no longer relevant, sometimes the very act of noticing their influence is powerful enough to break the spell. But at other times it is possible to have a wonderful insight, and then a week later find yourself returning to the same outdated pattern again. It is sometimes helpful to design a small ritual to cut the ties that bind with the past. Here is a ritual that you could try, but, if you can design your own, better still.

Take each of your outdated beliefs or attitudes one at a time, and write them in big letters on a piece of paper. Slowly read what you have written, and then gently tell yourself that it was useful at the time, but it has served its purpose and you now want to let go of it. Find different words to give yourself the same message several times. The final step is to physically destroy it – for example, by scribbling over it, scrunching the paper into a ball, tearing it into small pieces, cutting it up with scissors or burning it. After you have done this, write a few reflections about what it felt like in your journal.

Exercise 3

Notice when your beliefs are limiting you, or holding you back in some way. Choose one of these beliefs, and, in order to examine its history, start with a word cloud or word list. Write fast and intuitively, putting down any word that feels associated with the initial belief. Collect as many words as possible, but don't attempt to put them in any order or hierarchy. Then you can start investigating what memories some of these words trigger for you. Be compassionate towards your younger self and allow this investigation to detach you gently from your outdated beliefs. Afterwards write a few reflections about what it felt like in your journal.

JOURNAL EXAMPLE

It was our last term at college before we graduated. Three of us took our sandwiches into the grounds, and sat in the warm sunshine to have lunch and chat. We started talking about a recent lecture on building up your private practice after graduation, with ideas on websites, advertising, special offers and so on. M liked the idea of giving introductory talks to the public, and he had ideas about where to hire a room and how to advertise to get people to come. As he talked about it, he became more and more enthusiastic and D gave him further ideas and suggestions. Then D turned to me and asked if I would be doing talks as well:

Me: 'Me? No way! I don't do public speaking.'

D: 'Why not? It seems a good way of spreading the word.'

Me: 'A good way of telling them to bring their rotten eggs and soggy tomatoes! I don't want to give them target practice, thank you!'

They laughed, as I had intended they should, and I went on: 'As I see it, it's a lot of work for little reward. Give me modern technology any time. I'm going to build up my practice through my website.'

M was a little offended: 'I think we are more likely to get clients through face-to-face contact. Then people can build up trust in you.'

I realised that I had gone too far: 'Sorry', I said, 'I'm sure giving talks is the best for you, but it doesn't suit me.'

There was silence for a while, while we enjoyed the sun. Then D said softly, 'It seems to me you've got big issues around public speaking. Where does that come from?'

I felt a sense of implosion, of inner collapse, of my breath emptying out of my lungs too fast. Much as I wanted to avoid the topic, this was a sure sign that I had issues I needed to investigate. I muttered some reply, but made a promise to myself that I would do some reflecting this weekend.

I decided to begin with a word cloud (see Figure 5.2).

Figure 5.2 Word cloud used as a part of self-reflection

The images that come up for me while writing these words are my experiences at school.

- At junior school we had to take it in turns to read out loud from the reading book. I could read well enough in my head to understand the page, but reading out loud brought with it all the traumas of mispronunciation. Afterwards, in the playground, the clever kids would laugh at me and call me stupid.

- As teenagers we were made to study Shakespeare, and, although I loved the poetry of it, I hated the class read-throughs, when we were all given parts. I can remember the blushing humiliation of being unable to pronounce unusual words, uncertain whether to stumble through them or ask for help.

- My parents wanted me to audition for the school play. I suppose they thought it would build up my confidence and it did, although not in the way they intended. I made myself very useful backstage, helping to build sets, adjust costumes and apply stage make-up to the actors.

I have decided to counterbalance these unhappy memories with a list of positive experiences:

- At college I have become used to joining in big group discussions.

- When I worked as a waitress, I had to explain the unusual words on the menu to our customers.

- When it was Dad's birthday, I made a speech in front of the family.

- When the old lady was trying to get off the bus, I shouted out to the driver to wait before closing the doors.

- When we do small group work at college, I have occasionally been the person to report back to the main group.

REFLECTIONS

I'm beginning to see there might be a difference between public speaking when it means having to be accurate with someone else's words and public speaking when I could have a chatty session with a small group of people over a cup of tea. This is beginning to look more possible, but I need to do more work on it.

Using humour

Just about everyone has moments when they are supposed to be discussing something serious and intense, and they suddenly abandon all seriousness and play with the absurd. It can happen in small groups when one person's quick wit sparks comments from other people like fireworks going round the room. It can happen when you are doing a routine job such as household cleaning or driving, and a sudden irreverent thought or image jumps into your mind.

The self-reflective journal is dedicated to self-development and can become very intense. But there are no rules to say that it cannot be playful as well, and using fun can lift the spirits in the moment, and make rereading a pleasure. Humour is also a very good antidote to negativity. Moon (2006), writing in *Learning Journals*, points out that there can often be a deeper value in working with the absurd:

> When there is to be discussion on a problem or issue, ask learners to develop absurd comments or solutions if it is a problem and to write them in journals. It is amazing how often these absurd comments/pieces of writing contain wisdom that would not otherwise be evident. (p.157)

The value of having fun is enormous. It provides relief from any task-based objective, it develops a sense of humour as well as the imagination and it enables spiritual expansion. Play is how children learn, consolidating experiences, rehearsing for the future, extending the imagination and making sense of their world and their relationships. This can equally apply to adult learners who need cheerfulness and fun alongside critical thinking.

There are many different ways of using humour in your reflections, although, if your tutor or supervisor is to see your journal, it might be advisable to label it as such in case they misunderstand humour as disrespect – for example, by writing, 'I am going to push these ideas to absurd levels to see what it will reveal.'

Exercise 1

Think of a specific relationship with a client, colleague, friend or family member. You are going to do a visualisation about them, so sit comfortably with your eyes closed and your feet on the floor. Breathe deeply for a few minutes and, when you are ready, visualise that you are alone on a desert island. In your mind, look around you and observe the island: is it rocky or sandy or green with foliage? Then see yourself in the scenario: what are you wearing and what are you doing? Finally, introduce the other person: what are they doing and what are they saying to you? Push your visualisation towards the ridiculous. You can grow wings if you wish, or swim like Neptune under the water.

When you have finished, jot some notes about your visualisation into your journal and add your reflections.

Exercise 2

Choose one of the machines that helps you in your life – for example, your car, your computer, your phone or your washing machine. With modern technology, most probably all of these contain a mini-computer and are something of a robot. Choose a name and a personality for the machine, using humour and metaphor, and avoiding reality. The name you choose should include a quality or description, such as 'she who must be obeyed' or 'the cat's best friend' or 'powered by hot air' or 'the green hurricane'. Now imagine this robot talking to you. What would it say?

Exercise 3

Think of a work colleague who pushes your buttons, irritates you, bullies you, upsets you, makes you jealous or provokes any other strong emotion in you. Write about them, pushing your imagery into the absurd. While doing this exercise, avoid negativity. Your current task is not to write about how awful this person is, but to lighten up your thinking by bringing some humour into the story. Afterwards, reflect on what you have discovered.

JOURNAL EXAMPLE

I am so FED UP with my team at work. We seem to be incapable of having a simple meeting. They are continuously sniping at each other, firing off sharp comments and oneupmanship. I feel as if I'm coming into a war zone every week! I hadn't thought about it as a war zone before – let's see if I can pursue this image and discover where it will take me.

E comes into the room with a smile on his face and you'd think he was going to be pleasant, but when he throws his heavy rucksack onto the floor you know that it's not full of books: it's loaded up with hardware. He never goes anywhere without a couple of grenades in his bag, and there are handguns sheathed under his coat. W is a DIY man, clever with his hands, always ready to rustle up a Molotov cocktail or turn your headphone cables into a garrote.

He can hack into any computer, and you know for sure that he can make your mobile phone explode in your hands. P walks softly like a smiling tiger on velvet paws. She is highly trained in martial arts and her toned body is ready to pounce at any time, while tucked into her boots are sharp knives and across her back she carries a rifle.

We have not come here to have a meeting. It is a subtle game of poker that could explode at any second into a fight to the death. How can I save my skin? I do not have the others' fighting skills or their firepower.

Underneath the table I quickly switch on my pocket music player, turn the volume up high, push back my chair and leap onto the table. I dance fast, beating out tattoos on the table, proud like a Spanish flamenco dancer. The others are motionless, mesmerised by the music and dancing. The music slows and becomes more lyrical. From my position dancing on the table, the others look very small and calm, and for the moment it appears I have tamed them (no disrespect intended).

REFLECTIONS

As soon as I wrote that my colleagues were sniping at each other, my thoughts rapidly morphed from war zone to action film, and I could see each of them as a powerful adversary. It's interesting that I did not want to give myself fighting skills, but I gave myself other skills that my colleagues can respect. It's almost as good as the tarantula myth, where those bitten by the deadly spider have to compulsively dance the Tarantella to effect a cure.

My insight is that a complete change of focus is what's needed. The team members are very guarded, ready to protect their territory and their boundaries. They have their opinions and prejudices and are unprepared to see each others' points of view. But it is all a sort of hot air. If I give them a new focus where they are in unfamiliar territory, they shrink down in size.

Appreciation of good things

Sometimes the journal can become a repository for negative emotions, such as anger, irritability, disappointment, doubt, sadness or guilt. These negative emotions can expand and influence your thoughts, and, although an outpouring of emotion (see Chapter 3) is a healthy discharge, repeated airing of such emotions can entrench you in them.

The antidote to this is to work with appreciation or gratitude. There is a small but important difference between these two. Gratitude implies a previous struggle that has been surmounted. For example, consider the phrase, 'I am so happy and grateful now that I have...' These words are sometimes repeated as a visualisation tool, with the aim of attracting something new into someone's life. But at the same time as asking for this new quality or possession, the phrase echoes the current lack, suggesting, 'I would be grateful if it came now because I didn't have it before.' On the other hand, appreciation is taking delight in what is already there. You can feel appreciation for the beauty of the day, the kindness of a stranger, the taste of a meal, the smile of a baby or the softness of your cat's fur.

Try to introduce a short list of appreciations into your journal on a regular basis. You can appreciate friends, family, colleagues, clients, acquaintances and strangers. You can appreciate them for things as small as a smile or a moment of kindness. You can appreciate yourself for your work, your achievements, the condition of your body, your health or your relationships. You can appreciate your house or your apartment, with the shape, patterns and comfort of your furnishings. You can appreciate nature, the town you live in or the transport system. You can appreciate everything that you taste, touch, smell, hear or see.

I was working with a student who kept writing in her journal about her six-year-old daughter. She tried her utmost to express love towards her little girl but she kept being irritated by her daughter's clumsiness and bad behaviour. I suggested that she write a list of between five and ten appreciations of her daughter every evening. It was very effective because within a few weeks she was much more tolerant, and the child's behaviour began to improve.

Try some of these opportunities to appreciate.

Exercise 1

Next time you take a car ride when you are the passenger, spend five minutes appreciating some aspect of everything you see as a stream of consciousness. According to what you see, you could appreciate the trees planted along the roadside, the person who is driving the car, the colour of the car, other drivers, houses, billboards, buses, a glimpse of someone in a red shirt, flowers by the wayside, an aeroplane with a vapour trail, a couple walking hand in hand or flag fluttering in the wind. Give them all some of your loving appreciation. It is even more fun if you do this when sitting on a bus, because you can choose to appreciate something about everyone who gets on and off the bus.

When you get home, write as many of your appreciations as you remember into your journal.

Exercise 2

Think about your favourite grumble, or your pet hate. This is something that continually irritates you, even though it never seems to change. Write in your journal a list of the positive aspects of the issue that you normally grumble about. Be careful not to include any of your usual negative thoughts, which will easily come to mind because they have been aired so often. Just write about what is good about it – even if it only happened for a fleeting moment – and write with a cheerful attitude and positive intention.

JOURNAL EXAMPLE

I have been grumbling a lot about my office, which is not the large, organised, clutter-free space of my colleagues.
  Appreciation for my office:

- I really appreciate the big window that catches the morning sun in the winter, and brightens up our grey days.

- I love the big comfortable armchair that I purloined from the tenth floor office.

- I love the sense of peace that I get when I sit down to do some work at my desk.

- I like being able to eat my sandwiches at my desk.

- I really like the way all my books are to hand.

- I am thrilled with my fast, modern, efficient computer!

- I'm very fond of the old palm plant that sits peacefully near the window and has been there as long as I remember.

- I like the way my colleague puts her head around the door and asks me if I would like a cup of coffee.

- I have a secret love of stationery, which I indulge in my office with paper of different weights, textures and colours, and loads of gorgeous pens.

- I love writing my journal every morning in my office!

- It's wonderful to have somewhere quiet and peaceful to make phone calls to clients.

REFLECTIONS

It wasn't so difficult to appreciate my office after all, but what surprised me was that the word 'peaceful' came up three times. I have grumbled about my office so many times without realising the value of its peacefulness.

CHAPTER 6

CREATIVE AND ART JOURNALS

Clouds changing shape
drifting across blue skies
peaceful day

Self-reflection is defined in Chapter 4 as a regular, deliberate examination of issues as they arise. It is a way of increasing self-knowledge for the purpose of self-development, with further benefits to clients and/or the profession. Many people find that they can self-reflect within their journal, which provides a safe space for them to explore their thoughts, beliefs, values, attitudes or feelings. More than this, many people enjoy the process of linear thinking and the formal expression of their issue in words.

The advantage of using written words is that they form a long-term record of the issue, which can be described from both a factual and an emotional point of view, with an analysis, a conclusion and an action plan. This is helpful if the journal is going to be presented to a critical friend, tutor or supervisor, when words provide the common language that the other person can understand.

However, this raises the question of why self-reflection should be bound up with words, especially when some people are right-brain thinkers and would get more out of being creative and non-verbal. Modern Western attitudes tend to encourage left-brained, logical and analytic thinking, but who is to say that self-knowledge cannot be achieved through non-verbal reflection? A possible disadvantage of non-verbal work is that it can be difficult to communicate, lacking the lingua franca of words. This becomes a problem if it is intended to be shared with a critical friend, supervisor or tutor. Another disadvantage is that it can be ephemeral, expressed in the now with no physical form to survive it.

I suggest that creative or non-verbal self-reflection is valid, but it needs a brief summary in writing as a record of the creative process and reflective insights. This opens up opportunities for rereading and further learning at a later date. If the main work of self-reflection is non-verbal, the journal itself becomes a record book or log book containing the briefest of jottings, memos and notes interspersed with drawings, photos and so on. Non-verbal work can also be recorded through larger artworks, video or audio recordings. Together, the written notes and visual clues will be enough to remind the journal writer of the process and what was learned.

All self-reflection is introspective and contemplative. Written reflection often begins with a description of events and often ends with an action plan. Creative self-reflection frequently begins with emotional discomfort and ends with emotional resolution. Because resolution has been found, the attitude changes on a deep level and a specific action plan is not always necessary. Creative reflection could be labelled a different paradigm, allowing the journal writer to feel (rather than think) their way to a conclusion.

I suggest it's not so much a different paradigm as a method to cut away the wordage to get to the heart of the matter. As a supervisor of practitioners, my experience is that, when I encourage them to reflect creatively, it produces fast and effective change in the now without the need for an action plan. Witnessing their creative reflections, I can easily see that change has happened, without the need for words. It is evident in the 'ah-ha moment', followed by the relaxed body language and the smile. It is confirmed in the long-term feedback from the practitioner.

However, creative work is often not practical in an educational setup. As a teacher of reflective practice, I prefer students to write in a logical, thinking style so that I can follow their progress. I want to see concrete evidence of reflection, leading to a carefully chosen action plan as a mark of their intention to change. I need to look at numerous assignments, and do not have the time to ponder over another's creativity.

I find myself supporting both rational and intuitive self-reflection. I suggest that we leave aside preconceptions and prejudices about which is the best way to self-reflect. Different styles suit different people – whether they are left- or right-brain dominant, for example – and their novice status or familiarity with self-reflection will also have an impact on their choice. A journal can use both styles according to the subject matter, the time available or the mood of the writer.

In Chapter 3, I queried how much a description of the issue can be relied upon as an accurate recall and how much it is the writer's story. People make stories out of their experiences in order to make sense of them. Perhaps all self-reflection begins intuitively with an act of creation, to be followed by greater or lesser amounts of logical analysis.

Different types of creative self-reflection

Taylor, writing in *Reflective Practice*, is enthusiastic about using different methodologies for self-reflection. She says, 'The more creative you can be in selecting means to suit you, the better it will be for you' (2000, p.57). However, she does make the point that there will still need to be some form of record of the creative self-reflection, which she says can be written in a journal or taped by audio or video recorder:

> Even though I think writing is an important means of recording your thoughts and feelings, it is not the only way to aid your reflection. I'm hoping that this news may come as a pleasant surprise if you're someone who has trouble writing things down... It is important that you keep a record of your practice stories for reviewing and this is possible through writing, audio taping, creating music, dancing, drawings, montage, painting, poetry, pottery, quilting, singing and videotaping. (p.57)

Here are some examples of techniques and aids for creative self-reflection. Most of these are discussed in more detail later in the chapter.

Using a voice or video recorder: Voice and video recorders are small, non-threatening and easy to use, so once you get over the initial surprise of hearing yourself say everything out loud, they can be a very fast and effective tool for self-reflecting. You will need to be conscientious about filing and labelling your recorded material.

Drawing or painting: Drawings and paintings are most effective if they are not too consciously realistic. Colours, patterns and lines are used to represent feelings, attitudes, values or atmospheres. A few notes or key words can be added at the time or later.

Photographs: A collection of photographs can be put together to represent moods, feelings, attitudes or values. The collecting up of these photos is intuitive, but afterwards they can be observed objectively to discover the less obvious themes.

Montage or scrapbook: A montage or scrapbook is a collection of pictures and words, cut and pasted to create an assembled image that expresses your issues, thoughts or feelings. It is an intuitive process of gathering together different elements and combining them as a whole.

Poetry: Poetry is a very precise and concise use of language, focusing on the rhythm, pattern, sound or mouth-feel of words. When you're writing poetry for yourself, it does not need to be written according to any formula or format – it just needs to appeal to you.

Singing, dancing, music making and mime: These are all expressions using the whole body, and they can be spontaneous or planned.

Playing with toys and bricks: Children's toys are chosen to symbolically represent people or objects. They are deliberately placed on a table in relationship to each other in order to recreate an event, dilemma or issue. This allows you to review the scenario from the position of an observer.

Using visual templates: Standard shapes, such as squares, circles, stars, apples, the sun or clouds are used to recreate aspects of an issue or event, together with words, arrows and lines.

Using charts and diagrams: There are a whole range of charts and diagrams that can be a very useful way of visually demonstrating the complexity of some issues.

Transformation through creative journaling

Initially there is the satisfaction of simply being creative and enjoying the process of working within a different medium. Beyond this, you might find that, while you are involved in doing something creative, you enter a different time-space reality, where you are disconnected from the real world and absorbed in what you're doing. When the inspiration flows, you often feel energised, focused, empowered or enthusiastic.

Immediately after completing the piece of work, you might feel a sense of peace and satisfaction. This might be followed by feelings of surprise at how it turned out, because during the act of creation there was no vision of the outcome. Sometimes the creator becomes disappointed with their creation ('I can't draw') – if this is you, then remind yourself that there should be no right or wrong, good or bad. The value was in the process, not the result. It all leads to greater learning both about the methodology of creating the artwork and about the inner process of self-understanding. This will gain added potency if you began the creative piece with the intention of self-development.

Creative self-reflection encourages intuitive leaps of understanding, because it does not approach the issue directly in the manner of written self-reflection. The act of creation, whether it is through artwork, song, poem, dance or anything else, accesses intuition, imagination, feelings and fantasies. Self-understanding can arise organically, with no apparent effort, from this rich soil.

Transformation through creative self-reflection is a feeling in the heart, in the gut or in the breathing. It is an inner feeling that the issue has released or changed, making way for something new. It is vague, intuitive and can be described as a knowing, but it is often beyond words. I have recommended that notes are made in the journal, as a record for the future, but it can be difficult to translate the felt-sense into language. The record is more likely to be a few notes describing the finished piece, or a pasted-in copy if it is something like a small drawing or poetry.

Getting in touch with your spirituality

There are numerous ways of getting in touch with your spirituality, but many of the great teachers recommend slowing down the business of everyday life and quieting the mind. This can be done through meditation, prayer, joining a retreat, yoga, breathing exercises or walking in nature, for example.

I suggest that becoming involved in the act of creativity is a similar experience. The value of becoming absorbed in the act of creation is that it is restful for the thinking brain, similar to meditation, and it provides a channel for unconscious knowledge and emotions to flow towards the surface. It doesn't matter whether the resulting artwork is a 'good' piece or not. What matters is the person's intimate involvement with the process of creation. From within this process, it can feel as if time slows down and all the day-to-day problems are forgotten. There can be a feeling of inner knowing, as if inspiration were flowing through the body directly into the artwork. The mind becomes quietened and negative emotions drop away, leaving a sense of contentment, peace or inner joy. There can be a sense of connection to the greater good. Even if this experience only lasts a few minutes, it will help reduce stress, and unconscious solutions to problems can rise to the surface. Then you will yawn, stretch, or look around like someone waking up from a nap, or coming out of meditation.

In the rest of this chapter, I give more suggestions on the different techniques for creative self-reflection. I hope these inspire you to try something different. Remember there are no right or wrong ways of working creatively – we just have different styles. Do a short reflection after each exercise.

The art journal: drawing and painting

The art journal has a physical presence in the form of a notebook or sketchbook, rather than being created on the computer. The type of sketchbook and quality of paper are chosen with care; often a large-sized format is used and even then it can extend beyond or overflow the book. Art journals often have extra material such as drawings, photos, photocopies or even three-dimensional items glued in. The art journal is expansive, intuitive, colourful and free-flowing.

At its most basic level, the use of drawings and artwork can add an exciting and dramatic element to any written diary or journal. Your eye is attracted to them before engaging with the text. Artwork will always enhance the written word, either through the visual impact of breaking up the text, or through increasing the level of creativity on the page, which, like a tidal wave, raises the standard of the writing. Don't limit yourself by any outdated views about your own artistic ability. If you can put lines on the page, you can draw, and the very act of frequently using drawings will make you more confident in doing them.

Even the simplest of drawings can give an immediate visual clue to the emotional content of the text. For example, you can use drawings of a smiling or frowning face as a sort of emotional thermometer in a journal. When an issue needs to be reflected on, the little frowning face will flag up the issue, and, when it has been resolved through self-reflection, it will return to a smiley face. Alternatively, stick men can be used, such as the cartoon (see Figure 6.1) showing how the burden of too much 'stuff' to carry can be relieved by regular use of a journal.

Figure 6.1 Stick men used to tell a story of too much to carry

Drawings can be an effective way of exploring your unconscious processes. You might think that you have no issues that you wish to write about, but if you start the journal entry with a free-form drawing, this can provide plenty of material to work with. This is a process of taking a line for a walk across the page, and allowing shapes or patterns to arise as they will. You might wish to analyse the resulting drawing if any specific images present themselves; alternatively, you might just focus on any feelings that changed or developed while you were drawing. You can then explore these feelings, try to identify where they originated from and make notes. Rainer (1978), writing in *The New Diary*, says:

> Some diarists use free drawings as they would free-intuitive writing to tap their inner consciousness. Such drawings might be called *maps of consciousness* – graphic images of what's in your mind. The process is like meditation. You relax and without

intent allow the pen to move where it will on the page. You let
your hand lead the drawing and see what it makes as it goes.
(p.83)

Starting your reflections with a drawing can lead comfortably to
writing about what you have drawn, and sometimes it is good to
go back to drawing again for the final conclusion or consolidation.
You can either do a fresh drawing or you can rework the original
drawing. Some might feel it would be wrong to rework the original
drawing, because this is like trying to rewrite history. But if you have
done some exploration of your feelings, you will be coming back
to it with a different attitude and a reworking will bring resolution.

Another use of artwork is to explore a particular issue. This is
not to produce a photo-like representation of the issue or incident,
but rather to use pen and paper to express the energy or the feelings
behind the issue. This can be done using blocks of colour, lines,
arrows, spirals and squiggles. An angry person, for example, might
be represented by a red circle with arrows and lightning strikes
coming out of it. Try not to be too literal while doing this and
allow yourself to follow your intuition. If you leave the drawing for
a while and return to it later, you might notice things that you had
not perceived while doing the drawing.

Using artwork for self-reflection is a process that becomes more
effective with practice. It relies on the trust that your unconscious
will have perceived facets of the situation that you did not register
consciously. Referring to the Johari window (see Chapter 1), however
hard you try to be fully present, everyone has blind spots. Allowing
yourself to relax and go with the flow of creativity gives your
unconscious mind an opportunity to express itself and can reveal
new information. If the new insights revealed are very surprising,
they can be verified by further conscious investigation.

Exercise 1

Consider the drawing (see Figure 6.2). It was drawn after a
clinic session. The people present were the homeopath (H),
the patient who was in her early teens (P), the patient's
mother (M) and two students who were observing the case
(S). There was a lot going on at the same time, so afterwards

the homeopath decided to express this as a drawing of the energy and vibrational atmosphere provided by each of the participants. She had already taken notes and made her own observations, but she wanted to explore the interconnections of the five people.

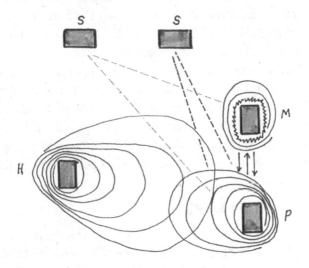

Figure 6.2 Diagrammatic illustration of five people in a room and their interactions

Spend some time looking at this drawing and note your observations and reflections about it.

Exercise 2
Collect up some paper and a variety of pens before you start, and take a few minutes to relax. When you are ready, choose a soft pencil and scribble with wide arm movements across the page. Take pleasure in the freedom of movement, and let the pencil go wherever it wants, at what speed it wants. When this feels finished, take your time looking over the scribble to see what emerges. Can you see patterns, machines, faces, people, animals, nature or anything else? Using pens or coloured felt tips, allow a picture to emerge from the scribbles, using the lines that are already on the page. Later, reflect on what you have discovered.

Exercise 3

Sit quietly for a few minutes, breathing deeply and simply enjoying being in the moment. Then consider a client or patient with whom you have worked recently (or observed if you are a student). As you bring your patient to mind, find a metaphor that would describe them – for example, a plant or animal, a vehicle or machine, a character out of a film or fairytale, or something else. No disrespect should be intended, but rather a desire to understand the patient at a deeper level.

Collect your favourite drawing paper and a variety of pens, felt tips or paint, and create the patient in their new role following your metaphor. See if you can push the metaphor further. When you have finished, leave it for an hour or so, and when you come back to it make some notes about what you felt while you were doing it and what you observe afterwards.

JOURNAL EXAMPLE

I did a drawing of the family group that I saw in clinic yesterday (see Figure 6.3). I wanted to see if I could discover more about the family dynamics. The parents were concerned about their teenage boy, who was rebellious. The father did most of the talking and at times he appeared overbearing. The mother said little, and gave the impression of being rather delicate, although very beautiful. The daughter sat very closely by her, sort of snuggling up to her.

I did the drawing thinking about the family and what they had said, and tried to feel how to represent them. The centre of the picture had to be the beautiful, delicate mother, whom I saw as a rose bush, with her children either side of her, and her husband as a tree.

Figure 6.3 Symbolic illustration of a family of four as plants

REFLECTIONS

- *The rose* is a strong and vigorous bush, well rooted in the ground – and it has thorns! Perhaps the mother is not so fragile after all.

- *The tree* is very protective, but it prevents the rest of the plants getting light and water. Perhaps the father is well intentioned and protective, but suffocates the others. This expands on my impression of him being overbearing.

- *The tall plant* on the right is the teenage boy. As a plant he is in the best position to receive light and rain, and he is vigorous, sexy and flourishing. Perhaps his rebellion is necessary so that he is not suffocated by the tree.

- *The little plant* is the little girl. I more or less ignored her in the interview and yet as a plant she is drooping. She is overshadowed and unlikely to get enough water.

I ignored her and maybe the family is also neglecting her in some way.

This gives me a lot to think about, and opens up my ideas about how to deal with this family. I need to do further observations to confirm what I have discovered through drawing.

The art journal: mixed media

The mixed media art journal takes drawing and painting one step further into a rich and complex representation. Working intuitively, the paper is covered with colour, pattern, shapes, texture, drawing, writing and print. The different media include watercolour, acrylic paint, permanent markers, pasted-in drawings, texts, magazine images or photos. These can be layered up slowly, providing a history of the process on the page.

The mixed media journal provides a hands-on, experiential session and demands a total involvement between you and your artwork. The act of creating the artwork is felt physically and emotionally. It can be used to express moods, feelings or states of being; or to describe a particular issue that happened at work or in clinic; or as a more expressive, creative form of the study journal. The act of recreating the study material in an intuitive way helps the writer engage with the topic on a visceral level in order to understand it.

According to Minton (1997), the majority of our learning is through visual stimuli. In *Teaching Skills in Further and Adult Education*, he says:

Since we experience 70 per cent of what we learn by using sight, visual images and presentation are very powerful aids to learning. They are usually more effective than sound alone. Most people's seeing skills are much more highly developed than their listening skills. (p.85)

Exercise 1

Sit quietly for a while with your eyes closed and your body relaxed. Breathe deeply for a few minutes and enjoy the feeling of the breath going down to the bottom of your lungs. Bring to mind a patient or client who is proving difficult at the moment. Ask yourself the simple question, what colour would best represent this person? If this person was a sound, what would that be? What texture, taste or smell would this person be?

When you're ready, gather up your sketchbook, paints, brushes and any magazine photos or clipart that might contribute, and create a mixed media page that represents your patient. Allow the page to develop intuitively. When you have finished, put it to one side for a few hours, and then return to it with fresh eyes and write some notes about what you notice.

Exercise 2

Take a piece of heavy paper, a paintbrush, some magazine clippings and three or four colours of acrylic paint. Allow yourself to work intuitively, and create a page that represents how you feel about one aspect of clinical practice. Acrylic paint dries quickly, so you can add layers of paint and include magazine pictures or text.

JOURNAL EXAMPLE

REFLECTIONS

A patient who has been with me for several years has left me a message that she is transferring to my colleague. She does not say why she is changing to another practitioner. I guess she is not satisfied with my treatment of her. I felt a whole mixture of emotions, leaving me feeling tense and stressed for the rest of the day, so when I got home I got out my paints (see Figure 6.4).

Figure 6.4 Mixed media artwork expressing sorrow at the loss of a patient

As soon as I started, the image of the butterflies came to me, and I used them as negative images as well as positive ones. I think this expresses very well my mixture of emotions. I was pleased that she's going, and sad that she's going, and furious and jealous towards my colleague. My inner and very irrational voice wanted to say that my colleague stole my patient. What's that all about? I have always found that when one patient leaves another one will come. This feeling of jealousy sounds similar to when a friend turns their back on you and makes new friends. I felt abandoned. I'm clearly in my Child ego state.

Thunderstorms appear on the page, expressing my anger. It's probably more comfortable for me to feel anger rather than guilt – as if I had failed this patient or she had moved on out of desperation. I almost wanted one more chance to try again. My instruction to myself is, 'Let her go with love.' I can forgive myself for not being able to cure her – I can forgive her for leaving me – I can forgive my colleague for taking her on. We are the three butterflies going towards a new future.

I will write to her a friendly letter, wishing her all the best for the future and offering to transfer the notes if that is what my colleague needs.

The scrapbook journal

The scrapbook journal or single page montage is often a colourful, vibrant mixture of journal writing, artwork, pictures and memorabilia that invites interaction with the reader. It frequently has a relaxed style, often deliberately mixing together the formal and informal in a fun and cheerful presentation. The additional material that is pasted in can include newspaper cuttings, pictures from magazines, photos, clipart, postcards, programmes and tickets from events, and much more. The pages themselves can be decorated.

For some people, 'scrapbooking' is an absorbing hobby. Their scrapbooks are beautifully crafted works of art, demanding a lot of time, money and careful planning. These scrapbooks are put together with the care and precision of a hand-sewn patchwork quilt, with all colours and textures carefully coordinated. They become an exquisite presentation for family history, family photos, friendship groups, yearbooks and so on. They can be decorated with stickers, stamps, cardboard shapes, alphabet letters, lace, wire, fabric, ribbon, beads and sequins.

For the scrapbooker, there is the quiet, contemplative enjoyment of compiling a carefully presented artwork, and the satisfaction when it is complete. These crafted scrapbooks are designed to be shown off to an audience, with each page carefully protected from dust and fingerprints.

The scrapbook journal has another character altogether. It is much less planned and less deliberate. It has energy and spontaneity and can be an illustrated version of the narrative journal. The pasted-in elements can have several different purposes. They can act as illustrations to brighten up the page, they can be a shorthand reminder of various events and issues, and they can be used as triggers for self-reflection. The scrapbook journal can contain printed copies of emails, thank you cards from clients, seminar notes, business cards from colleagues, newspaper cuttings or advertisements, as well as self-reflection.

The satisfaction of doing the scrapbook journal is often in its informality. In situations where a self-reflective journal is mandatory or strongly recommended, the journal writer can yearn for autonomy and independence. Doing a scrapbook version allows the writer to have fun and make up their own rules. There is the risk with a scrapbook journal that the reflection will not be as deep as it could be, so I suggest including the occasional reflective framework (Chapter 7) as necessary. The very nature of the scrapbook journal invites all the other styles of journaling to be included.

The variety and interest of the scrapbook journal encourages the writer to engage regularly with it, creating new entries and rereading old ones. For visual or tactile learners, it allows sensory stimuli alongside serious reflection. It can be equally creative as an art journal, but in many cases it is faster and more fun. Rereading happens automatically, because the differing weights and textures of each page provoke curiosity.

Exercise 1

Look through some old magazines and newspapers, and cut out a picture of a family group. You can interpret this as loosely as you wish. Paste the picture into your journal, and look at it for a few minutes. Then ask yourself the following questions and write your reflections in the journal alongside the picture.

- Why did I choose this picture?

- How does it make me feel?

- What does it remind me of?

Exercise 2

Create a collage 'word cloud', gathering together all the words that reflect your particular skill set. For example, the words that chefs might use to summarise their skills include timing, efficiency, steadiness, planning, recipes, flavour, hygiene and so on. Word clouds are often done on the computer, with key words in different fonts jumbled together within the cloud shape. You can do it like this if you wish, but you will probably have more fun with coloured paper, felt-tip pens, crayons, glue and scissors.

After you have finished your word cloud, consider whether you have any weaknesses in any of the areas you have identified. You do not need to criticise yourself but you can make some plans to enhance your skills in any area where they are weak.

Exercise 3

Put together a montage to represent the best of your past year. Imagine it is the end of the academic, financial or calendar year and you want to review and enjoy all that you have achieved.

You can cut out pictures and comments from magazines and newspapers, or you can look on the internet for any clipart that is freely available. You can print out complimentary emails from friends or colleagues, or include memorabilia such as train tickets, pictures from brochures or photos. If possible, include a photo of yourself taken within the past year. Spend some time collecting material for your montage and remember that it is a celebration of what you have achieved.

Your montage can be carefully scaled so that it fits within the journal pages, or it can expand into a wall hanging. Enjoy your time reviewing and celebrating the past year.

Exercise 4

Consider a hobby or project that you have been involved in over the past six months or year. Do a scrapbook journal entry or montage to represent what has happened and what you have learned.

Figure 6.5 is a journal example of a scrapbook page. This one is quite self-explanatory, but it need not contain so much information and could include more pictures or diagrams.

JOURNAL EXAMPLE

A full week in clinic

The Healing Centre

What did I do well?
- Fresh and focused with each new patient until Friday.
- Kept all my notes up-to-date and booked in future appointments.
- Very calm with Mrs X and her three children, who were all tired, restless and whining after school.
- Tactful with elderly Mrs Y who wanted to talk, talk, talk!
- Fitted in an emergency patient as well.

What didn't I do so well?
- Didn't give myself enough time between patients.
- Less energy and less concentration by Friday - beginning to droop.
- Forgot to return a patient phone call for three days.

From: Sara P
To: Annette J
Sent: Tuesday, May 01, 20-- 4:34 PM
Subject: Thank you!

Dear Annette,
Thanks so much for seeing my daughter Isabel at such short notice.
She is much better already!
With regards
Sara P

How do I feel?
- Mentally exhausted, worn out.
- Physically hyperactive, ready for more.
- Overwhelmed.
- Uncertain whether I did a good job, it's all a blur.
- Excited, positive, proud of myself.

Why did I take on so many patients?
I've never had such a full week - but I've never had the opportunity. There was a sense of excitement and pride that so many people wanted to see me. The Rescuer in me was happy to help. I even took on an extra case but then felt overwhelmed. Now I feel overtired but wound up. It's not a healthy state. Next time I will schedule in less patients and more time for me.

Figure 6.5 Scrapbook journal entry after a busy day

Using charts and diagrams

There are a rich variety of charts and diagrams that can be used for self-reflection. All these are visual demonstrations of how the different facets of an issue interconnect. Words are used as labels or headings, but not in a full sentence. The advantage of making a chart is that it simplifies the information and clarifies the issue. After it has been done, it remains in the journal as a quick and easy reference point. There will be added value if you write a few lines of self-reflection after doing the chart, as a memorandum of what you have learned.

Venn diagrams, pie charts, flow charts, bar charts and tree diagrams can all usefully represent different issues. Venn diagrams with interconnecting circles show how things overlap – for example, two or three different aspects of your work. Pie charts divide up the whole into proportions, and can be used to show how you spend your time at work or how you spend your money.

Tree diagrams demonstrate a specific type of network, showing how one factor can be divided up into numerous others. They can be used to show many diverse past influences and how they contribute towards the present, such as a complex timeline or family tree. For example, they can be used to chart your educational pathway, including schools, influential teachers and key achievements.

Flow charts show progression from one state to another and can be as simple as a string of beads or complex like an underground or subway map. They break down a process into the individual events or activities, showing the logical relationships between them. Each individual component is connected to others with arrows showing the flow. Flow charts can be used to identify all the steps necessary for doing a certain piece of work or achieving a predetermined outcome.

Mind maps or spidergrams start with a central issue and explode outwards across the page in every direction, identifying as many different connecting issues as possible. They can be used to brainstorm new ideas or stuck areas – for example, they can be used when you feel resistant to doing a certain piece of work, or have a mental block about doing something. The brainstorming process can open up new understanding.

Experiment with including more charts and diagrams into your journal. Try out some of the following suggestions, or invent new ones for yourself.

Exercise 1

Look back into your past and consider which people and experiences nurtured you and/or helped you become the person that you are. For example, you might (or might not) want to include your parents, siblings, schoolteachers, classmates, friends and work colleagues. You also might want to include certain books, poetry, movies, sports events or a single inspiring experience. Your environment might have influenced you, or the experience of travelling.

Put this information together as a flow chart, organisational chart or family tree. You might find there are some free frameworks on your computer or on the internet. Otherwise you can draw it free hand. Do not feel constrained by any particular style, and include drawings as well as written comments. If you're not keen on doing your own drawings, you can search the internet for free clipart that you can include.

Exercise 2

Think about how you divide up your time either within one day or within a seven-day week. How much time do you allocate to work, family life, chores around the house, leisure activities, looking after a pet, sleep or pampering yourself? Create a pie chart in your journal to show how your time is divided up. Write some reflections on what you have discovered.

If you are surprised or disappointed in the results, create a new pie chart to show an improved division of time, but do not be too idealistic. Design something that you should be able to achieve.

Exercise 3

Think about an issue that is bothering you at work, and write a short paragraph in your journal describing it. Then pick out two or three key words or a short sentence or two that you feel summarises the issue. Write these in the centre of a new page within a small circle. Write down as many ideas and connections as you possibly can from your key words, and write them as a mind map extending outwards in any direction from the original circle. Try to push the pace a little, and include everything that comes to mind even if it doesn't seem relevant at first.

When you have written as much as you can, put it to one side for an hour or so and come back to look at it with fresh eyes. You might find you want to add more things to the mind map at this point, or you might start having new insights into the original issue. When you have finished, jot down some reflections about what you have learned.

JOURNAL EXAMPLE

I have been trying to decide if I should do further training. It seems very expensive and will take up a lot of my spare time, but I suppose it will benefit me in the long term. I think I will do a mind map to see if that clarifies things for me (see Figure 6.6).

REFLECTIONS

I found I had a lot of questions, and there was certainly a lot of anxiety around the thought of further training, but it felt quite grounding to put it on the mind map and find some answers. Yes, I do have the time if I get myself organised. Yes, I can get a loan if I commit myself to doing the work and getting the qualification. Yes, I do have the commitment because I'm bored with my present job! As for worrying whether I am clever enough, it seems better to put that one on the backburner until after the open day, when I can meet with staff and students and ask questions.

Figure 6.6 Mind map used to decide about further training

Playing with toys and bricks

This method has been described extensively in *Inspiring Creative Supervision* written by the author and a colleague (Schuck and Wood 2011). It can be used by a supervisor working with a supervisee, but it can be equally effective if you do it on your own. Small toy figurines, animals and bricks are used to symbolise different aspects of the original issue. If you allow yourself to be quietly contemplative while you are doing this, the process of choosing toys and placing them allows you to access your intuitive or unconscious knowledge. Schuck and Wood (2011) write:

> This method of supervision gives quick and often unexpected results as it uses symbolic objects to represent people, their emotions and their interactions. It is a quick way to get at unconscious processes. Often once a supervisee has tried this method, even reluctant supervisees, they may opt for it time and time again. It cuts across the conscious processes and allows something new to emerge. There is an excitement and a playfulness attached to it, that makes it feel less like work and more like fun, encouraging the supervisee to return for more insightful sessions. (p.66)

Toy animals can include domestic pets, farm animals, wild and jungle animals, insects, snakes, fish, birds, butterflies and dinosaurs. Toy figurines can include figures from fairy stories and mythology, such as witches, wizards, knights on horseback, fairies or goblins. There can be figures from popular cartoon films, and characters representing different careers such as a nurse, fire-fighter, policeman, soldier, ballet dancer or film star.

When used for self-reflection, they can represent various people, different facets of the same person, objects such as books or machines, businesses or communities or something else. Each toy item is chosen because of its symbolic meaning, rather than its visual similarity to the original. Anything can represent anyone or anything. For example, a book can be represented by a reel of thread because of its never-ending nature, or it can be represented by a wise owl. A person might be represented by a toy car because they are always rushing everywhere, or by a dinosaur. Even as you read the word 'dinosaur', you will have preconceptions about the symbolic meaning for you.

No disrespect is meant to the original people or situation that you are representing. What you are reflecting on is your perception of how they appear to you and how they interact with you.

Once the toy figurines and animals have been chosen to represent the issue, they are placed in a constellation, showing the interaction between them. Bricks, blocks or even pencils can be used to show the boundary or lack of boundaries between these people and objects. Having put together the constellation, you will need a little time to come out of your contemplative, introspective state, in order to learn from what you have created. Turn away from it and take a few slow, deep breaths.

The next step is carefully to observe your constellation of people and animals. What can you notice about the toys that you chose? What can you learn from the positioning of the pieces? If you work with a critical friend, it is very useful to show your constellation to them, through a photo or video.

The final step is to experiment with making changes, and see what this feels like. Ask yourself gentle, undemanding questions, such as 'I wonder what it would feel like if I swapped this animal for that one?' Or 'Wouldn't it be nice if I could be more like this figurine in this relationship?' Make the changes and see what it feels like. If it doesn't feel right, you can always change it back. In my experience, changing a constellation can be very empowering.

Exercise 1

This is a light-hearted task to remind you of how useful animal metaphors are. Recall a time within the past couple of weeks when you took some exercise or played a sport. Rather than being literal about what happened in a factual way, remember your mood, or the mood of the people you were with. Remember the atmosphere, the weather or the conditions at the gym.

Now use some animal metaphors to describe your experience. For example, you can use established phrases where the animal is coupled with a descriptive adjective such as 'I felt as strong as an ox, but I was sweating like a pig,' or 'When I started running, I felt as free as a bird.' You can also invent your own animal descriptions, such as 'I went into the gym as cautiously as a cat in a new territory, but, meeting a friend, I started chattering like a parrot.'

Exercise 2

If you do not have access to a collection of toy animals and figurines, try this experiment. Gather together some small objects from your desk, pockets, briefcase or handbag – for example, you can find pen tops, erasers, bulldog clips, pencils, paper weights, coffee spoons, plastic cups, coins, hair clips, make-up containers or jewellery.

Remember a time when you had to do a really intense piece of work, when you felt under pressure and stretched intellectually. Choose two or three of the objects to represent the different facets of yourself at that time, and choose another one to represent the task you were working at. Add pieces to represent any other people that were influential at that time. Place the objects in a constellation that best delineates the conditions at the time.

When you have finished, turn away for a few minutes, then come back to look at it again with fresh eyes. What did you notice? Make some notes in your reflective journal.

JOURNAL EXAMPLE

I've been working in two clinics for two years now and I've been wondering whether it's time to drop the clinics and work from home. One of my clinics is just once a month and it is voluntary: I get loads of interesting experience there. In the other one, I work three days a week and they charge an extortionate amount for the room. But they have a receptionist and it's great working in a multidisciplinary practice. Am I ready to move on? I will use the animals to get my ideas started (see Figure 6.7). I have represented myself as:

- the green parrot (I am talkative, flying high, but frequently caged)

- the fire-fighter (I am quick thinking and good at solving problems)

- the brown dog (I like working in a pack; I'm loyal and housetrained)

- the black-and-white cat (I am fiercely independent, and prefer to walk alone).

Figure 6.7 Toy animals and figurines used to investigate changes in the work

The advantages of having some fire-fighter in my nature are that I am quick thinking, good at solving problems and I'm dedicated to my work. I work for other people, helping to put out their fires. My cat nature likes to be independent and walk alone, which means working from home would suit me. My green parrot clearly wants to fly high, doesn't like being caged and is ambitious to move on. Its talkative nature represents my abilities to advertise and get new clients. I'm also very chatty and friendly with clients, which makes a nice atmosphere for them. These are all positive qualities that should help me set up my own business.

Later: I have been rethinking about my chattiness with clients in the consulting room. I would like to think it is good, but am I trying to self-justify? A little bit of chattiness at the beginning and end of the consultation is fine, but the rest is their time and I should be listening, not talking.

My brown dog nature likes to work in a team and I can see this might be a problem, making me miss the busy clinic. Realising this helps me to decide that I should keep on with the voluntary clinic once a month. The advantage of the brown dog is that it likes routine, and this will help me keep organised with the stuff the receptionist normally does, as well as filing. I think it's okay to have both cat and dog in my nature as long as they both know what their role is. The cat, of course, is in charge.

The most unstable part of my character seems to be my green parrot, which will contribute towards setting up a business from home, but could fly off in all directions. Oh, I've just realised, it is me who has to put the parrot into the cage. The parrot's ability to fly off in all directions, it's repetitive talking and even its flamboyant appearance all need to be held in check because they are potentially my downfall. The biggest contribution of the parrot is its ambition and wish to fly high, so I'll let it out of the cage when I am making a website and advertising; but it needs to go back into the cage when I'm with clients.

If I make a new constellation of my four figurines, I would have the cat standing next to the fire-fighter, ready to go forward independently. The dog is on the other side of the fire-fighter, walking to heel. Out in front but to one side, there is the green parrot with pencils symbolising a cage around it. That feels good!

Mime and acting

Mime is a useful technique if the issue you want to reflect on has to do with relationships, such as the practitioner–patient relationship. Re-enacting the other person in the relationship gives you an opportunity to feel what it's like to be them and experience life through their eyes for a few moments. You can do this in front of a critical friend or supervisor, as a shorthand way of describing someone else. You can do it by yourself, as a way of remembering and reconnecting with another person. Either way, the main focus should be on the non-verbal communication. The priority should be acting out the body language and facial expressions, although you can include non-verbal noises such as 'hmm-hmm' and, if you feel it would help, you can include language as well.

This technique is used by supervisors in the helping professions, when the supervisee wants to discuss their client. Re-enacting or miming the client (who is absent) brings their presence into the room. I usually recommend working with the first five minutes of the consultation unless there is any particularly intense time during the interview that should be explored.

If you are working on your own, take a few minutes to recall a recent interview or conversation you had with another person. Then place an empty chair to represent yourself, while you enact the other person. If it is helpful, you can sit in the empty chair and give your replies. Keep as accurately as you can to the conversation as it happened and do not be tempted to rewrite history. Your aim is to understand the other person and why they behaved as they did, which in turn will help you reflect on your own behaviour.

Other uses of mime or acting can be as a sort of role-play or rehearsal for an interview or conversation, or as a learning tool. For example, if you are preparing for an interview, or you are studying one of the helping professions, miming alongside the new words, phrases, techniques or skills can help you absorb the information on a deep visceral level.

Exercise 1

Remember a movie or TV film that you have watched several times and really enjoy. Choose one of the main characters in a key scene, and re-enact or mime that person to see what it feels like being in their shoes for a few minutes. Then do the same mime in front of the mirror to observe yourself. What have you learned? Write some notes for yourself in your journal.

Exercise 2

Next time you have a disagreement or argument with someone at work, and after you have cooled down, take five minutes to mime their behaviour. You can take an empty chair to represent yourself in this argument, and try to be honest about how the other person would have felt. Don't try to justify your own point of view, but just take a few minutes to feel the confrontation from their side. Write about this in your journal.

JOURNAL EXAMPLE

I meet with my two colleagues once a month, so that we can give each other supervision on our work. I was trying to describe my patient, when one of my colleagues suggested that I mime her. It was a truly interesting experience!

I am sitting on the edge of my seat, with a very straight back, but this is not from rigidity – it's more a sort of excitement. I'm very expressive with my face, and I use a lot of extreme adjectives as I talk. I use my hands a lot to express my feelings, and I run my hands through my hair. Suddenly my spine collapses as I start giggling, covering my mouth like a child.

REFLECTIONS

There are patterns of strength and weakness, excitement, communication, sexiness, allure and childishness.

What surprised me were the polarities of strength and weakness, allure and childishness. I had not been so aware of them while I was sitting in front of my patient, but acting it out really helped me understand her. She is more vulnerable than I had perceived. At the time of the interview, I was mostly aware of her excitement and sense of fun. My drawing of her shows even more childishness and an actor's comic mask (see Figure 6.8). Her expressiveness, both verbally and non-verbally, feels as if it is put on for the entertainment of the audience.

Figure 6.8 Drawing done after acting a patient's body language

CHAPTER 7

REFLECTIVE FRAMEWORKS AND MODELS

The still mirror
of trees in the lake
broken by ducks

Reflection can be done in many different ways, ranging from right-brained, intuitive methods through to left-brained, structured techniques. Different methods or styles suit different people, but the choice also depends upon the aim and intention of the journal writer. Sometimes it is appropriate to let thoughts meander, in order to see what arises. At other times there are work-related issues that need to be thought through carefully in order to make changes to tasks, productivity, relationships or outcomes. Working within a specific model or using a reflective framework can provide structure and ensure that each aspect is looked at in turn.

Reflective frameworks, templates and models clearly signpost how the writer should direct their thoughts, taking them through a step-by-step process of reflection. They create a safety net, reducing the chances that the writer will avoid what they don't want to see. They are good for the beginner to reflective practice because of the question-and-answer format in many of them. They also work very well as part of the mature reflective journal, because they encourage deep self-questioning.

Following a structured model has many advantages. It reminds the writer to look at different aspects of the issue, covering many different bases. This ensures a more holistic approach to self-reflection.

It gives the writer independence and autonomy to resolve issues on their own, without the help of a supervisor or manager. Many structured models include an action plan, paving the way forward. They can be used with a variety of different issues – for example, to:

- implement a clinical audit in order to do a reality check on existing tasks, systems or outcomes

- make considered decisions and plan strategically for the future

- reflect on a specific issue, incident or dilemma that needs to be dealt with promptly

- clear past issues and emotions that are having an impact on current conditions or relationships

- consider an issue through different viewpoints to gain perspectives

- appreciate the complexity of most situations and take ownership of one's own part in them.

The disadvantages of structured models or frameworks are that writers can feel they should follow the steps rigidly, or that they should follow them in a linear fashion. This might limit the reflection, preventing a more creative expansion in many different directions. The ah-ha moment of realisation can be lost in the pursuit of logic. Johns (2009) writes in *Becoming a Reflective Practitioner*:

> I am wary of cyclical or stage models…because they suggest that reflection is an orderly step-by-step progression. Reflection is not a neat movement between different stages or cycles. To view it in this way suggests a mechanical flow through discrete stages. Reflection is complex, whereby the mind engages all stages… The risk is that practitioners will fit their experience to the model of reflection rather than using the model creatively to guide them to see self within the context of the particular experience. (p.50)

This is a timely reminder that models should be used creatively, engaging the right-brain ability to look at the bigger picture as well as the logical left brain. Johns' (2009) own Model of Structured Reflection has a whole series of cue questions designed to stimulate reflection from many different angles. It is designed specifically for the reflective practitioner and, although it can be used within the journal, it probably works best as a supervision tool in a face-to-face session.

My suggestion is that you experiment with working with different structured models to find out which you prefer, which is the most suitable for your current issue and which you learn the most from.

Transformation using models and frameworks

Many reflective frameworks are carefully structured to take the writer through a gradual process of reflective questioning. They are left brained, logical and analytical, and they are very effective in getting the writer to understand themselves better and in opening up the blind spots.

All the models and frameworks require time and careful consideration. They do not flow as freely and as comfortably as other types of journal writing. They demand some digging into thoughts, feelings, attitudes, motivations and values, and sometimes they reveal new truths that are surprising or even startling. It is not always an easy process, and the insights can be complex or painful.

The benefit is that, as you begin to understand yourself on increasingly deeper levels, there is a feeling of liberation from outdated attachments. You become more true to yourself, choosing your own attitudes and values rather than adhering to inherited ones. In understanding yourself, you begin to understand and become more compassionate towards other people.

Here are seven different models or frameworks for self-reflection. None of them is better than the others, but it is worth trying out different techniques to see which you feel most comfortable with and which you learn the most from – not always the same thing.

Making SMART plans

The journal is a useful place to explore your future wants and needs in a personal or professional setting. For some people, planning is an easy process because they can clearly see what they would like from the future. They decide what they want, visualise it and take steps to ensure that it comes about. For other people, planning is a more difficult process, either because they were content where they were, or because they are restless for change but do not know what it is they want. Others need planning skills in order to complete their CPD plan.

Plans for future change work best if they are done with SMART objectives. This mnemonic stands for Specific, Measurable, Attainable, Realistic and Time Bound. Using a SMART framework forces you to be very clear and specific about what you want and then asks how you're going to go about it, when you'll do it, and how you're going to measure the success of it. This provides structure and boundaries which in turn keep up the energy of the project, making it easier to achieve.

There are four steps in planning the future:

1. *Identify all aspects of your current position.* Clarify what you do, what is effective and how much you are enjoying it.

2. *Investigate future options.* Explore what you might like to happen in the future and what appeals to you as an improvement.

3. *Choose your new goal.* Decide on a realistic new goal to aim for.

4. *Create practical steps to achieve your goal.* Choose several practical and SMART strategies to help you achieve your goal, and use your journal to chart your progress.

Four different exercises for planning the future are suggested here.

Exercise 1
Ask yourself a series of questions, beginning with:

- Where am I at this point in my career?

- What is good and bad about my current situation?

- What would I like to change?

- Where do I see myself in one or two years' time?

- What would I like to have achieved in five years' time?

- What do I need to do now in order to achieve that?

- What further training or research do I need to do?

After you have answered these questions, reflect on what you have learned about yourself.

Exercise 2

Create a mind map showing all the different elements of your current work. A mind map is an excellent way of showing the complexity and inter-connectedness of everything you do. It is often useful to use a range of colours, to represent the various themes, or to represent your emotional reaction to each facet of your work.

When your mind map is complete, ask yourself the following questions:

- What is there too much of – that I would like to reduce?

- What is there too little of – that I would like to increase?

- What is missing?

Add these to the map, using a new colour or highlighter. Then ask yourself the final question:

- What do I need to do to make this happen?

Exercise 3

If you have a clear vision of what your goal is, a fun exercise is to create stepping stones leading from where you are now to where you want to go. Start off with writing your goal in large letters at the top of the page in your journal. Then spend some time pondering on the different steps or strategies you could take in order to achieve it, and write a list of 12 or more underneath the goal heading. Out of this list, choose a realistic six, considering your resources of time, money, contacts and so on. For example, if you are self-employed and your goal is to build up your work, your stepping stones might include upgrading your website, writing an advertising feature in a local newspaper, doing a visualisation, networking with other people in similar work, buying a money plant (*Crassula ovata*) to symbolically encourage more money to come towards you, or creating a special offer for new clients.

Next you should provide yourself with a small pile of large (A4 or similar) sheets of paper and some broad nib felt pens. Write your goal in large letters on the first piece of paper together with the date you want to achieve it by. Then write out your six chosen strategies, each one on a new piece of paper. Now lay them out on the floor, with the goal at the furthest distance from you, and the stepping stones in a timeline leading towards it. Take your first step onto the first stone, and declare out loud what you need to do to achieve this step. Walking slowly, stand on each stone in turn, saying what you need to do until you reach your goal.

The second part of this exercise might not seem necessary because you have already written everything in your journal. But making it into a physical journey, so that you walk across your stepping stones, builds up your confidence and embeds your plan.

Exercise 4

Review your work and how it is going this year. To simplify the review, write it into two lists with the headings, 'What is going well?' and 'What is not going so well?' When you have completed these lists, write a conclusion about what you have discovered and what you need to do. Decide on an action plan, and make each facet SMART.

JOURNAL EXAMPLE

My supervisor has asked me to review where I am at present and to begin to write a personal development plan for the next year. I will start with two lists, in order to clarify where I am at the moment:

WHAT IS GOING WELL?

- My counselling practice is going well and I'm getting enough clients every week.
- I really like working from my office at home.
- It suits me to be self-employed.

- I have just started working as a supervisor at the Centre. It's very new for me but it seems to be going well.

- A colleague (W) wants me to write an article with him for the newsletter.

WHAT IS NOT GOING WELL?

- I feel out of my depth supervising someone who is older than me. I feel as if I haven't had enough training or experience.

- I think I want more supervision work but I feel ambivalent and anxious about it – so do I really want it?

- My computer crashed and I felt helpless. I had to organise going to my friend's house to get my emails.

- Client AM – she likes to play Victim and last time she came I felt myself slipping into Rescuer role. I need more supervision on this.

CONCLUSION

- I need to investigate further supervision training.

- Once I have done further training, I can have a rethink about building up my supervision work.

- I need to make a contract or working agreement with W before I start writing the article with him.

- I need to be very strict about computer back-ups.

- I need to take client AM to my own supervisor.

- I need to explore my issues about supervising someone older.

HERE ARE MY OBJECTIVES IN 'SMART' DETAIL

1. I would like to do the supervision training within the next year. Modules cost £350 each, and I will have achieved it when I have got the certificate for completing all four.

2. I will arrange to get together with W and make a working agreement about writing. We can find the time within the next three weeks, and meet in a café. The cost will be a cup of coffee, and we will have achieved it when we are both satisfied with it.

3. I bought an external hard drive (£80) and I have started PC back-ups already. I must write reminders in my diary at the end of every week and tick them off when I have done them.

4. I can take client AM to my next supervision session booked for two weeks' time. It will be the usual fee, and I will have achieved it when I have made an action plan about what to do with AM.

5. I would like to work on my issues around supervising someone older, using my reflective journal. I think I will do a written dialogue with myself. I will do that later this week. No cost. I will have achieved it when I have got to that ah-ha moment.

SWOT analysis

A SWOT analysis (credited to Albert Humphrey 1960s–1970s in Stanford University) evaluates your Strengths, Weaknesses, Opportunities and Threats, which are written in a box divided into four equal parts, or four segments of a circle. The value of it is that it combines brainstorming with structure. Unlike the cyclical models, it can be filled in in any order as the thoughts arise. It can be used for decision making or for planning a specific project, and thoughts can be expressed as sentences, phrases or single words.

If it is used for decision making, the SWOT analysis helps you identify the arguments for and against a choice. If it is used for planning a specific project, it can help you identify whether your plan is viable or not, and it takes you forward into choosing areas for development or making an action plan.

At the top of the page, write your goal, objective or question. This needs to be clarified before you start. Then divide the page into four quarters or segments, with the headings of 'strengths', 'weaknesses', 'opportunities' and 'threats':

- Strengths are the personal resources, knowledge and experience that you already have, such as skills, techniques, values and attitudes.

- Weaknesses are the skills and attributes that you lack, placing you at a disadvantage, such as negative work habits or anxieties that prevent you taking on certain roles.

- Opportunities are the external chances and openings that will help you to achieve your goal, such as new experiences, training or new technology.

- Threats are the external obstacles that could make trouble for you, such as changing technology or competition from other people.

Exercise 1

Imagine that you are self-employed as a CAM therapist with a middle level practice, neither too busy nor too quiet. You are asked by a colleague to take over her practice for five months while she takes maternity leave. Her practice is local to you and also middle level in quantity.

Make a SWOT analysis, in order to decide about taking on the practice. You need to consider many different aspects, such as whether your colleague attracts the same sort of patients as you do, how often her patients will expect to see you, what she charges, whether she will write an introductory letter for you, what happens if her patients want to transfer allegiance after five months, whether her patients are willing to travel to your clinic or whether you are willing to travel to her clinic, your increased income and correspondingly increased workload, and so on. Consider as many different aspects as you can under the four headings, in order to resolve the dilemma.

Exercise 2

Think back to when you decided to take on the job you have at the moment. What factors influenced your choice? Put them on a SWOT chart. Alternatively, consider the pros and cons of having further training, and put them on a SWOT chart. Reflect on what you observe.

Exercise 3

Choose a current or previous dilemma, where you have found the decision-making process very difficult. Make a SWOT analysis of your dilemma. Then reflect on what you have discovered.

Strengths	Weaknesses
I won't feel so isolated if I'm meeting up with others.	I can get shy with new colleagues.
I've got a big front room where we can meet.	It might be difficult to get in touch with everyone.
I used to belong to a support group, so I know how good they can be.	I don't know the protocol. Would I have to provide tea and biscuits?
I could email my old group facilitator and ask her advice.	I'm not very good at organisation and planning.
	There wouldn't be a facilitator.
Opportunities	**Threats**
We can learn from each other about treatment plans for difficult cases.	How do I get everyone to sit down together and agree what we want?
We can practise treatments on each other.	The others might expect too much of me as if I was teacher or facilitator.
We can share information about seminars, workshops, etc.	We might end up arguing about the purpose of the group.
We can share magazines and journals.	We might end up with someone really bossy who tries to take over the group.
We can locum for each other when we go on holiday.	What happens if only one or two people turn up?

Figure 7.1 SWOT analysis used to help decide about setting up a support group

JOURNAL EXAMPLE

Should I set up a support group for fellow practitioners to meet once a month (see Figure 7.1)?

REFLECTIONS

I am torn between my rose-tinted image of how good it could be and my fear that it could all go horribly wrong. I can see us in a very happy routine of meeting up once a month and supporting each other. The main threats in my mind are of how to set up a working agreement – the getting started bit. I would like to email my previous group facilitator to see if she'd be willing to give some advice. She lives too far away to join us, but she might have some suggestions about what we need to discuss. Perhaps I could get in contact with just one or two colleagues and get them on my side before inviting everyone for a preliminary meeting.

Doing a clinical audit

Clinical audit is a process of measuring clinical practice against agreed standards, and implementing change to improve patient care. It is a systematic review, focusing on some aspects of care or the whole care package with the aim of checking good intentions against reality. Explicit criteria are used to measure the audit and changes should be implemented to improve services afterwards. If possible, there should be a second audit after the changes have been put in place. Clinical auditing has been formally incorporated into the healthcare system of many countries, including Great Britain, and it can be carried out by any private practitioner who is involved in the treatment of patients.

Without a clinical audit you can imagine that you are providing the best service for your patients or clients, but unless this is measured there is no knowing how effective you are in reality. If you are a self-employed practitioner, you might feel overwhelmed at the thought of doing an audit, but if you choose a small aspect of the work it need not take up too much time and it may indeed be fun. For example, an audit can be done around phone messaging, sending out information, greeting a client at the door, the last five minutes of a session, or keeping records up to date.

There are four steps to an audit:

1. *Identify best practice.* Decide upon the ideal standard of service, referring to the relevant code of ethics, etc.

2. *Set up the audit and carry it out.* Make sure the audit tests reality against specific criteria that come from best practice.

3. *Review the audit.* Analyse and review the audit results.

4. *Implement changes.* Put in place changes to improve practice, and plan a further audit to test these.

Audits should be SMART. The topic needs to be specific, so you need to be very clear about which aspect of your work will be checked and measured. This is not as difficult as it sounds, and all you need to do is ask yourself, 'What do I want to achieve and how will I know whether I have achieved it?' Your goal should be both attainable and relevant. The aim of a clinical audit is to improve your work practice by one or two notches. It does not need to turn it inside out. However, the audit does need to be practical, within your time and budget limitations. You also need to choose the timeframe within which you will do the audit; four to six weeks is usually sufficient, but it does depend upon the throughput of work.

If you have chosen to audit your clients' perception of your work, an effective method is to design and print a questionnaire. First of all you should do a reflective piece in your journal, identifying what is best practice and what will provide maximum client satisfaction (not necessarily the same thing). Refer to your code of ethics, which will give guidelines for good practice. If you still find it difficult to identify good practice, remember those times that you have been a patient or client, describe the service you received and notice where it was lacking. From this journal work you can compile a questionnaire to hand out to all your clients within your chosen timeframe.

If you have chosen to audit your own behaviour in relation to your work or your clients, a good method is to design and keep a tick chart in your reflective journal. As usual, you should first identify what is best practice within the area that you want to audit. Maybe this has already been made explicit by your ruling body, but if you're self-employed you can write your own best practice list. For example, if your focus is going to be greeting a client at the door, your best practice list will include the following.

- Answer the door promptly.
- Know your client's name, and greet them politely.
- Introduce yourself.
- Guide them to the clinic room and show them where to sit.

If you're going to make a chart, you can have these criteria listed down the side, and the name of every client who comes to the door listed along the top. Then you can check your behaviour against each client.

Exercise 1
Choose one aspect of your work, and write a best-practice list about it. Refer to your code of ethics and any other occupational standards that have been published by your governing body. Also consider your own personal values.

Exercise 2
Do a mini-audit for a week on one aspect of your private life. For example, you could choose your early morning routine, including checkpoints around time, self-care and efficiency, as well as issues around getting distracted, organisation, tidiness and so on. Reflect on what you have discovered.

Exercise 3
First, identify your strengths and weaknesses in your work, and then decide which particular area you want to focus on. For your chosen focus, find out what the different aspects of best practice would be and list these. When you are satisfied that you have the criteria that you want to work with, make up a tick chart with all the different aspects of best practice that you want to test yourself against. Complete this chart over a month or six weeks, and then do some self-reflection on what you have discovered.

JOURNAL EXAMPLE

I am a self-employed homeopath. I have identified that my strengths in practice management are:

- dealing effectively with phone enquiries
- keeping my website up to date
- making introductions and signposting at the beginning of a consultation
- building up a good practitioner–patient relationship
- supporting a patient between appointments
- keeping my patient records up to date.

I have identified that my weaknesses in practice are:

- actively advertising for more patients
- working with children
- finishing a clinic session gently and effectively when I myself am feeling tired.

I have decided to do an audit on finishing a clinic session to help me clarify what's going wrong, and then choose an action plan. In order to do this, I have identified best practice as:

- telling a patient that we're coming towards the end of the clinic session
- asking if there is anything else the patient would like to say
- explaining to them my conclusions, avoiding jargon, and checking they understand
- negotiating a treatment plan with them, and booking in the next appointment
- asking if they have any questions
- thanking and praising them and taking the fee
- showing them to the front door.

I made a tick chart with these criteria in my journal. I have kept it for a month, filling it in after every patient appointment.

REFLECTIONS

I found that knowing I would have to fill in my chart improved my overall performance. I was particularly good at explaining my conclusions and negotiating a treatment plan. I scored 100 per cent when it came to thanking and praising patients. However, I frequently forgot to ask if they had any questions.

I think that this links strongly with my tiredness at the end of a consultation. I put so much into the relationship that, when the time is up, I just want the patient to leave. My resistance is around giving them the opportunity to have a last word or to ask questions. By then my energy level has gone down, and I don't want to talk to them any more.

My action plan to deal with this is twofold. I have decided to give myself 15 minutes between patients, so that I feel completely refreshed. I will also conclude each consultation ten minutes before time, to create a space in which to offer them the opportunity for further thoughts or questions.

Three-step reflection

The first cyclical model for self-reflection that I am giving in this chapter provides structure, logic and key questions to trigger reflective thinking. The cyclical format encourages further cycles of reflection.

Borton's (1970) developmental model for reflective practice has a deceptively simple, three-step framework, asking the questions, What? So what? and Now what? These questions are always asked in sequence and the last question refers back to the beginning again, completing the cycle.

What? The first question sparks off a multitude of different reflective questions, such as what happened, what was my role, what were my intentions, what were my actions, what were the consequences, what were my feelings or those of others?

So what? The second question encourages questions such as so what does this teach me, or imply, or mean for me, so what else could I have done, so what is my new understanding of the situation, so what broader issues arise? Ask this question as many times as is necessary to investigate all the different implications.

Now what? The final question takes us forward into the future with questions such as now what should I do for the benefit of myself or other people, now what should I do to break this cycle, now what are the broader implications of this, now what are the consequences? Ask this question as many times as necessary.

Below are several different exercises to give you some ideas about how the three questions can be applied in different circumstances.

Exercise 1

Imagine a new patient comes for an appointment, saying that they have heard wonderful things about your work, and that they are expecting magical results. You explain that every case is different and you cannot promise miracles, but they persist in repeating the testimonials they have heard. You feel uneasy about being put on a pedestal. Continue reflecting on this scenario, following the three-step reflective cycle, and repeating the questions until you have covered all the options.

Exercise 2

Think of a small child whom you know very well, such as a sibling, son, daughter, cousin or neighbour, and imagine that a similar child comes to you in the clinic. You give the child toys and books to play with, and while the mother is talking the child accidentally-on-purpose breaks something. You notice but the mother does not. Reflect on what happened using the three questions, What? So what? and Now what? Repeat each question several times.

Exercise 3

Think of a critical incident that happened at your clinic. This would be an incident that made you stop and think, because it made you uncomfortable, irritated, sad, frustrated or anything else. With the question, What? describe what happened in a factual way. Then ask the question, So what? and go on asking it as many times as necessary until you have written about all the implications and consequences of the original incident. Finally, ask the question, Now what? as many times as you can until you have investigated all the possible action plans.

JOURNAL EXAMPLE

WHAT?

I have a private practice as a counsellor, working from my office at home. The telephone has two numbers and two distinct rings, one for my private life and one for my business. The phone rang at 9 p.m. and, mistaking the ringtone for my personal line, I picked it up. Unfortunately, it was the client who started with me last week, desperate for contact. As soon as I answered the phone, she poured out all her problems, talking fast and intensely. I was so surprised and overwhelmed that it took me several minutes to realise that I had to stop her talking, and to explain that I had picked up the phone by mistake. I apologised and reminded her of our working agreement, that I only work face to face, and that she had an appointment booked for next week.

SO WHAT?

I was really surprised that I had made this mistake and picked up the phone. I was expecting a phone call from my daughter, and I had been watching TV, feeling very relaxed and slightly sleepy. I wasn't concentrating on the ringtone – I just picked it up. This surprises me because normally the first ring of the phone makes me sit up and concentrate, listening to which line is ringing. I must have been more sleepy than I was aware of. I was so shocked at the consequences of answering the phone that I think I will never again forget to listen to the ringtone before I pick up.

SO WHAT?

It feels very unprofessional, and I am irritated with myself for making such a basic mistake. I exposed myself to a complete lack of boundaries by a) answering the phone at that time of night, and b) listening to the client talk for several minutes, because I didn't feel I could interrupt her.

SO WHAT?

From the client's point of view, I can guess at a rollercoaster of emotions: unhappiness that made her decide to phone me even though it was late, relief that I answered and she could talk to me, and then something like hurt, disappointment or indignation when I interrupted and said I could not talk. It's the sort of situation where clients feel let down and don't come back. If I had let the phone go into the answering service, she could have talked to her heart's content without being cut off by me.

NOW WHAT?

I feel I have a choice, either to wait until our next appointment and explain the situation to her face to face with further apologies, or I can write to her soon. I don't think I can phone her to apologise, because that will imply that she can, after all, have a phone session – and then I will have broken my boundaries again. I would prefer to speak to her face to face, but that is next week and in the meantime there is the risk that, if she feels offended, she won't return. So I am left with the option of email.

NOW WHAT?

As it was my mistake, I can offer the client an appointment sooner in the week, and I can consider giving her a small discount on the next appointment as well.

NOW WHAT?

I would like to double-check the literature that I send out to clients, to make sure that it is quite clear that I do not do phone sessions, and I don't work in the evenings after 8 p.m. I need to keep my boundaries clear.

NOW WHAT?

I'm still left with feelings of embarrassment, and wanting to tell myself off for my stupidity. My inner judge is working overtime. In order to forgive myself, I need to bring in my nurturing parental self. I can remind myself that this is the first time I have made this mistake; that normally I have good boundaries and I am professional; that I explained and apologised when we were on the phone; and that my shock at the whole episode will help to prevent it ever happening again.

Classic reflective cycle

The classic reflective cycle was first outlined by Gibbs (1988) and has subsequently been used by teachers, students and professionals in many walks of life. It takes the reflective writer through six different stages, starting with a basic description and progressing through deeper levels of understanding to an action plan. It is cyclical, encouraging the writer to go into further cycles of reflection.

Gibbs' (1988) reflective cycle is more prescriptive than Borton's (1970) model in that it directs the writer with specific questions. These enable you to reflect deeply about the issue, approaching it from different angles. The six different stages are as follows.

1. *Description*: What happened?

2. *Feelings*: What were you thinking and feeling?

3. *Evaluation*: What was good and bad about the experience?

4. *Analysis*: What sense can you make of the situation?

5. *Conclusion*: What else could you have done?

6. *Action plan*: If the situation arose again, what would you do?

The first two stages take you from the objective to the subjective, and the evaluation at stage three reminds you that there are good and bad sides to every experience. The analysis invites further investigation, perhaps into your past experiences, to explore what formed your current attitudes and values. It can also direct you to theory such as that written about in Chapter 1. The conclusion allows you to round everything off with a summary of your new understanding and a broader look at what else you could have done. When the issue has come from clinical practice, the conclusion can be quite complex and far from black and white.

The main weakness of this reflective cycle when applied to the healthcare sector is the final question: '*Action plan*: if the situation arose again, what would you do?' When working with people, the same issue very rarely arises again so forward planning in this respect is not helpful. However, this does not prevent a practitioner having an action plan in the sense of, 'What will you do now?' or 'How can you prepare for the future?'

Exercise 1

As a way of dipping your toe in the water, try working with the first three stages of the classic reflective cycle. These take you through objective and subjective, positive and negative, and have been suggested as exercises elsewhere in the book. Remember an incident when you were at school or college when either you were bullied by other children, you became a bully, or you witnessed bullying.

Description: What happened? Write an objective description of what happened, like a historical document, or a report from a policeman in court.

Feelings: What were you thinking and feeling? Write two separate paragraphs, one about your thoughts and one about your feelings. Both should be from a subjective point of view.

Evaluation: What was good and bad about the incident? Evaluation means weighing up positives and negatives. Write two separate paragraphs, one about what you did well, or the positive outcomes of the incident, and one about the negative outcomes or what you did not do so well.

Exercise 2

Choose for your topic an incident in clinic that you find you were mulling over days after it occurred. Write about it in your journal using the classic reflective cycle.

JOURNAL EXAMPLE

DESCRIPTION: WHAT HAPPENED?

We started case taking at the polyclinic at the beginning of the third year at uni. My first three cases went well, and this was my fourth case. I walked down the corridor to reception to collect my patient, and when he stood up I saw he was tall and wearing a suit. I introduced myself and took him back to the clinic room. I started to take the case, filling in the questionnaire, but went into a sort of panic attack. I looked down at my notes and pretended to read them, trying to breathe deeply and get control over my fear. I looked over at the supervisor, and she took my hint and asked a couple of questions. Then she politely asked me if I wanted to ask any more questions and I found I could take over again.

FEELINGS: WHAT WERE YOU THINKING AND FEELING?

It wasn't so bad when I collected my patient from reception, but it got worse and worse during the case taking. My mouth was very dry and I felt I was making a mess of things. I felt really panicky and stopped hearing what my patient was saying. My palms were sweaty. I wanted to run. I felt so relieved when my supervisor took over for five minutes.

EVALUATION: WHAT WAS GOOD AND BAD ABOUT THE EXPERIENCE?

It was good that I was polite and calm when I collected my patient from reception. It was good that he was calm himself. I was lucky that my supervisor realised what was happening and gave me five minutes to regain my self-control. Once I got through the case taking and started the acupuncture treatment, I felt a lot more confident.

It was bad that I should get so panicky with this particular patient. He is my fourth patient, after all. It's never happened to me before like that.

ANALYSIS: WHAT SENSE CAN YOU MAKE OF THE SITUATION?

The feeling that I wanted to run shows me this was a classic fight or flight reaction. It was caused by a rush of adrenaline, but inappropriate because there was no visible danger, just a mild-mannered patient.

I wonder if it was because this was the first time I have taken the case of a male patient. But the argument against this is that I observed many male patients when I was in second year. I think it was the fact he was in a suit rather than jeans. He was a really nice man, but my first impressions were that he was serious, formal, intelligent and probably critical.

I used to have a boss who was tall and wore a suit, who would mock me on a good day and be bitingly sarcastic if I made a mistake. He was very judgemental and made everyone feel small. He was in critical Parent mode and I was definitely in fearful Child, trying to keep underneath his radar. In clinic I felt the same: very small and very young, as if I was going to get told off.

In writing that, I have suddenly remembered that this did happen when I was small. The Christmas after Grandma died, Grandpa came to stay. He was always a formal sort of chap wearing slacks and a jacket, and he questioned me about school, what had I done and what had I learned? I remember feeling completely blank and frightened, unable to respond. To my eyes he seemed incredibly tall and critical. He was probably only trying to be friendly in his own way. In the past he had left the socialising with the grandchildren to Grandma. He must have been missing her, poor man.

Thinking about my relief when my supervisor took over, I can refer to the drama triangle. She was definitely my Rescuer, while my patient was (in my distorted view) a Persecutor. In expecting to be told off, I became Victim.

CONCLUSION: WHAT ELSE COULD YOU HAVE DONE?

We had a discussion about it at the end of clinic and the supervisor said we could ask for a private word with her, which would take us out of the consultation room for a few minutes. But she would still ask us to go back to the patient and finish the session.

If I had recognised earlier that I had imagined the patient to be a critical Parent while I was in Child mode, I might have been able to change that to Adult–Adult.

ACTION PLAN: WHAT WILL YOU DO NOW?

The first thing I want to do is find some photos of Grandpa, and try to recall lots of good memories about him. I don't want one Christmas to trigger panic attacks every time I see a tall man in a suit.

In future I shall do some breathing exercises before clinic, and remind myself that patients come to the clinic because they are unwell. They have chosen to come to a student clinic, so they are aware that we are in a learning process and there might be the odd hiccup. I can try to approach all patients on an Adult–Adult level. When this particular patient comes back for his follow-up, I will make sure that I am knowledgeable and well prepared, so that there is nothing to be anxious about.

The Ladder framework

The Ladder framework was first introduced by Schuck and Wood (2011) in *Inspiring Creative Supervision*. It is a framework that takes you step by step through six reflective questions to an action plan. Similar to the children's board game of Snakes and Ladders, it reminds you that reflecting on one issue can take you up the ladder of understanding, while another issue can slide you back down again. The slippery slide might take you back to the original starting point, but it is more likely that the next ladder will start slightly higher up with the knowledge gained the first time round.

There are six steps to this cycle (see Figure 7.2):

1. What are the facts?

2. What are your feelings?

3. What were your fantasies?

4. What were your strengths and weaknesses?

5. What have you learned?

6. What needs to change?

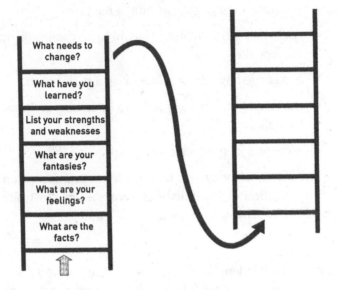

Figure 7.2 The Ladder framework for self-reflection

This framework allows you to separate your dispassionate description of events from your emotions, and encourages you to explore your fantasies about the event, however illogical or biased they might be. In using the word 'fantasies', I'm not writing about pleasant daydreams about your patient, whether sexual or otherwise. I am referring to the prejudices that come like a semi-translucent veil between the practitioner and patient in the consulting room. Even the most caring practitioner can slip into prejudice more often than they would like. In clinic a mythology about certain patients can easily arise (see Chapter 3). Exploring your fantasies can produce some interesting insights into why the experience developed as it did.

Try out the exercises below to work with your fantasies or prejudices.

Exercise 1

Spend a few minutes listing all your positive and negative thoughts, prejudices and fantasies about one or all of these people:

- A young teenage girl carrying a baby.

- A mother whose child is having a screaming fit in the supermarket.

- A teenage boy sitting slumped on a park bench.

- An elderly man who appears to be talking to himself as he walks.

- Someone jogging around the park.

Now ask yourself why you have those assumptions. Can you see any parallels or dissimilarities between your own life and the assumptions you have about these people?

Exercise 2

Choose an incident from your work and, writing in your journal, use the Ladder framework to investigate it. See what you discover about yourself.

JOURNAL EXAMPLE

WHAT ARE THE FACTS?

A woman phoned up to make an appointment for her daughter, who is 22. I asked if the daughter was actually interested in coming for homeopathy, because I don't like working with people who are resistant. The woman replied that her daughter wanted to work with me, but she was a schoolteacher and could not make phone calls during the day; when she got home she would be too tired. Her problem was extreme fatigue, probably post-viral fatigue. I asked if they had been to the doctor, and she said that their religion prevented them from taking conventional medication.

On the day of the appointment, the mother arrived by herself, even though it was half term and her daughter would not be at work. She said that she wanted to explain the background of her daughter's situation without her there. I felt uncertain about this so I asked if her daughter knew she had come. The woman said, 'Oh, she doesn't mind me talking about her.' She proceeded to tell me about the strict religious upbringing given to all her children, and described her daughter's illness.

WHAT WERE MY FEELINGS?

I was uncomfortable with the woman coming on her own, to talk about her grown-up daughter behind her back. I was pretty certain that the daughter did not know about her coming. I was shocked at the description of what was (to me) a repressive upbringing. I felt sorry for the girl and angry at the mother for treating her daughter as if she was still very young. I felt very prejudiced against the mother and her religion.

WHAT WERE MY FANTASIES?

I felt there was something underhand about the whole thing. I was pretty certain that the mother was telling lies. I thought the mother was very controlling. I felt I could not trust the mother, and imagined that the daughter also could not trust her. I wondered what had caused the daughter's symptoms of extreme fatigue and I speculated that the condition came from repression and loss of freedom.

WHAT WERE MY STRENGTHS AND WEAKNESSES?

These are all my strengths: at the initial phone call I made it quite clear that I would need to meet the daughter and discuss her symptoms with her. At the interview, I told the mother that I would not be able to prescribe until I had met the daughter herself. I told her I would have to charge for both appointments. All in all I was outwardly calm and professional, and stated my boundaries in a gentle but firm way. I made another appointment to meet the daughter later in the week.

My weak points are that I became embarrassed in front of the mother, so I couldn't make the most of the one-to-one xinterview with her. I felt awkward because I did not understand her religion and I couldn't assess whether her behaviour was the social norm or not. Usually I am quite comfortable about asking gentle questions about topics or attitudes that I have not met before. I have to admit that I was impatient for the interview to be over and the woman to leave.

WHAT HAVE I LEARNED?

Recognising my own embarrassment has been helpful. I think a lot of this came from my shock at the controlling behaviour, and subsequent fantasies that the mother was lying and untrustworthy. With these thoughts and feelings going on, it was almost impossible to get the information I needed.

WHAT NEEDS TO CHANGE?

Before the next appointment I can research the religion on the internet, to fill in some of the background. When the clients come, I don't need to be shy about asking the woman or her daughter whether this level of mothering for a 22-year-old is normal in their community. The main issue is not how I view the mother's behaviour, but whether the daughter finds it caring or controlling. I need to investigate what brought on the chronic fatigue, and I need to do this without prejudice.

Other People's Shoes

This is another model designed by Schuck and Wood (2011). It is a cyclical model, reminding us to walk a mile in someone else's shoes before judging them. The value of a cyclical model is that it invites you to engage in a second round of reflection, deepening the learning. The disadvantage of any cyclical model is that it can persuade you to follow the steps and answer each question in the correct order. This might suit some people but for others reflection is a more organic process, with answers to the questions coming up in any order.

The Other People's Shoes model begins with the separation of objective and subjective observations, and as it progresses you are invited to look at other people's viewpoints. At first it might seem difficult to imagine another person's experience, but you probably know far more than you realise. Looking at an issue from someone else's point of view takes you right out of self-justification and gets you to consider it from a very different perspective. This can open up interesting insights. See more about other people's viewpoints in Chapter 5. There are six steps to this framework (see Figure 7.3):

Figure 7.3 The Other People's Shoes model for self-reflection

Exercise 1

If you don't want to work through the full framework, here is a short exercise in looking at an incident through other people's viewpoints. Imagine a busy supermarket on a Saturday afternoon. A young woman with two small children and a large amount of shopping in her trolley has been held in the queue for too long. The children are fractious, and she is fed up, but the queue doesn't seem to be moving forwards. Suddenly she explodes, shouting first at her children and then, when a middle-aged man tries to intercede, shouting at him as well.

Rewrite this scenario from the point of view of the mother, one of the children, the middle-aged man, the cashier and the old lady who is at the front of the queue holding everyone up.

Exercise 2
Think of an issue that you had with another person, perhaps a confrontation with a work colleague or someone at home. Write about this in your reflective journal, using the Other People's Shoes framework.

JOURNAL EXAMPLE

WHAT ARE THE FACTS?

It was a staff meeting towards the end of term. My boss and four others arrived on time, someone was off sick, and another tutor and I both arrived late. I had been detained by one of the acupuncture students wanting to discuss her assignment. She was one of the more aggressive and awkward students, and it turned into an impromptu tutorial. However, I felt the value of spending time with her, and by the end of ten minutes she had a couple of excellent insights.

I hurried through the building but I was still last to get to the staffroom. My mind was full of the breakthrough with my student, and I made a light-hearted comment about working overtime. My boss replied with a long and angry speech about how everyone ought to arrive on time, and it was inexcusable to be late. I felt myself stiffen up, and I started to argue back, taking the exact stance that my aggressive student would have done in the past.

WHAT ARE YOUR FEELINGS?

I went through an absolute rollercoaster of feelings, starting with exasperation with my student for choosing a bad time; then pleasure that she was prepared to talk about her assignment quickly and efficiently; then excitement when she got it, leading to my inappropriate light-hearted comment in the staffroom; then anger at my boss's long angry speech.

I still feel irritated with my boss, whom I feel is very unfair, because she is not student centred and was not prepared to listen to my little success story.

WHAT SKILLS DID YOU HAVE OR LACK?

I think that I used a lot of skill with the student, getting her to think fast and effectively. I think I negotiated my way round her potential aggression very well. However, when I was shouted at by my boss, I lost all my negotiation skills and just wanted to defend my position.

IMAGINE OTHER POINTS OF VIEW

I think the student was pleased to have one-to-one attention. I want to focus my reflection on the people at the staff meeting.

My boss: 'I have just had a memo from the higher powers about time and resource efficiency, and if anyone looks into this room and sees that we are 15 minutes late and still haven't started the meeting, then I will get in trouble. If a student asks for a spontaneous tutorial, the tutor has to consider if the timing is appropriate, and suggest another time if necessary.'

My colleague who was also late: 'I was late because I had to make a phone call, but I'd better keep my head down because the boss won't accept that my private life is as important to me as my work life.'

The four colleagues who arrived on time: 'We managed to arrive on time, so why can't everyone else? All this is wasting time and, if the latecomers could have just come in with a polite apology, we could have started the meeting.'

WHAT ARE YOUR INSIGHTS?

I was able to talk to my student on an Adult–Adult basis, and make the ten-minute tutorial very effective. At the same time, in choosing to be late, albeit with an excellent reason, I was acting out my own inner rebellious Child. It's interesting that this particular student often acts like a rebellious child, and I wonder if I picked it up from her. Imagining my boss's point of view has shown me clearly that I could have rescheduled the mini-tutorial. I knew this on one level, and tried to get away with it by making a joke, and then became angry out of defensiveness.

I still think that my boss should not have shouted at me as soon as I walked through the staffroom door, but I think I was very provoking, arriving late and making a joke.

HOW DO YOU GO FORWARDS?

After all, my boss is my boss. If she makes rules about us arriving on time, then I should listen to her. Just because my student often behaves aggressively towards me, I shouldn't parallel this by behaving the same way to my boss. I think I should write a brief email to my boss, apologising for wasting her time. In future, I must remember to reschedule if students ask for mini-tutorials at the wrong time.

CHAPTER 8

VISUALISATION

Winter bonfire
patterns of curling smoke
creating dreams

Visualisation is a technique of creating something within the mind either through thinking about it or seeing it with the mind's eye. Like the art journal, visualisation uses creativity, spontaneity and intuition, and can involve all of the senses. The primary tools for doing the work are the imagination and the emotions.

Visualisations can be done quickly and spontaneously, but they can be more effective with a short meditation and serious intent. They integrate well into other forms of journals and can be spoken, written, drawn or created in some other way. In a logical, systematic journal, the writer might prefer to write out a full description of the visualisation. In a creative journal, the visualisation can be represented by drawings, charts and collages, as well as brief notes. Visualisations can be hand drawn or created on the computer.

I consider that there are three main types of visualisations that can be used in a journal. Creative visualisation can loosely be termed a goal-setting tool, which uses the power of the imagination to create new and desirable outcomes. Exploratory visualisation is a method suitable for exploring the unconscious and opening up blind spots. Maintenance visualisation helps the writer build up self-esteem or clear out unnecessary anxieties and brain clutter. These three types of visualisation focus on the past (exploratory), the present (maintenance) and the future (creative).

Transformation using visualisation

Creative visualisation is a deliberate and conscious use of the imagination as a tool to actively construct what is wanted from the future. It is a gentle way of taking action rather than leaving the future to good luck or fate – and the benefits are many. Even if it doesn't produce results, the process of visualisation includes focusing your mind and becoming clear and assured about what you want, all of which are empowering and raise self-esteem. Added to this, there is the possibility that by focusing clearly you can influence future outcomes.

Many writers suggest that everyone is visualising all the time. Losier writes, in *Law of Attraction*, that it doesn't matter if you're remembering, pretending, daydreaming or observing. Anything that you focus on with time, energy and imagination will act as a creative visualisation and attract more of the same, like a magnet: 'I attract to my life whatever I give my attention, energy and focus to, whether positive or negative' (2007, p.7).

If this is so, you have a very powerful tool for implementing change. Focusing on the positive can at least alter your perception of your environment and life circumstances, so that you feel good about what you have at the moment. Beyond this, creative visualisation can attract money, possessions, work, nourishing relationships or well-being into your life. On the other hand, continuously focusing on negative or unwanted scenarios can prolong them or make them chronic.

The law of attraction suggests that it is necessary to turn the thoughts and attention away from any current negative reality and focus only on present or future success to gain more success. This is the difference between perceiving your glass to be half full or half empty.

The second form of visualisation, which I'm calling 'exploratory', is a good technique for uncovering blind spots. This refers to the Johari window (see Chapter 1), which suggests that we all have areas in the unconscious that we do not know about. Sometimes you can uncover blind spots through diligent self-questioning using the reflective journal, and sometimes they can be effectively revealed through working with a critical friend or supervisor. Exploratory visualisation can access your unconscious surprisingly fast and reveal interesting new insights. It can be used to discover and subsequently release some of your past stuck feelings and attitudes.

The third form of visualisation, which I'm calling maintenance, is useful to de-stress and build up self-esteem. Stress rarely comes from external causes alone. It is most often compounded by overloading your mind with negative thinking, anxiety and limiting beliefs. It might feel as if these thoughts and anxieties are uncontrollable, but with clear visualisations and solid intention they can be reduced considerably.

Because all the three types of visualisation are done using creativity and intuition, it is a softer, gentler way of working. The polar opposite would be the reflective framework (Chapter 7) which is a very precise, hard edged, rational way of working. Frameworks have clear boundaries and can ask you to think about certain issues in turn. With visualisation there are many different ways of going about it, and it accepts that not all answers can be found by following a logical process.

Transformation through visualisation can be felt in the short term as a feeling of liberation in relinquishing the task of working hard. It allows you to hand over to the unconscious, go with the flow, and trust that what is revealed will be useful. In the long term, it can initiate profound changes in both inner thinking and objective outcomes.

How to do a visualisation

Visualisation takes 10 or 15 minutes and it is both playful and relaxing. It does not require specialist techniques or knowledge. I suggest three simple steps to visualisation:

1. Have a clear and honest intention of what you want to achieve, and do the visualisation with commitment.

2. Do the visualisation from your non-thinking mind, accessing your intuition and spontaneity.

3. With creative visualisation, let go of all your expectations *after* you have completed the visualisation. You have done all you need to do. At the most you can allow yourself a low-level curiosity about how it will manifest.

- For exploratory visualisation, let go of all your expectations *before* you start the visualisation. Allow yourself to be open to whatever is revealed.

- For the maintenance visualisation, finish with a cleansing ceremony.

When I am facilitating a visualisation for other people, I guide them through a short relaxation and meditation session to quiet both body and mind, which will make it easier to access the unconscious. As a facilitator, I want them to get into a state where the mind is thinking more slowly in a slightly dreamy, meditative or restful state. This is a deliberate closing down of the thinking brain in order to access intuition and spontaneous ideas or images. When you are working on your own, there are several different ways of accessing this state.

Relaxation and meditation: Sit on a chair with both feet on the floor or sit cross-legged on the floor, with your eyes closed or looking at something calming. Listen to your breathing and any other small noises that you can hear around the building or outside. Be aware of the ground under your feet, and the weight of your body being supported by the chair or the floor. Let all your muscles relax. After a little while, take one deeper inhalation, and let it out as a sigh. With the next few breaths, let all the little muscles in your face and neck relax with each out-breath. Enjoy the feeling of sitting quietly. If any thoughts arise, put them aside and return to listening to your breathing. You are now ready to start the visualisation.

Being creative: If you enjoy being creative, this is an active way of accessing quietness and intuition. Spend a little time quietly gathering all the materials you might need, such as paper, pens, paints, glue and so on. Sit and look at these materials in pleasurable anticipation, and then let your hands rather than your brain take the decision about what you will work with. Usually at this point you are ready to do the visualisation, and there will be a smooth transition between preparation and physically creating your visualisation. You can do a drawing, painting, montage or any three-dimensional work.

Using exercise: Exercise is an ideal way of getting into a quiet and non-thinking state. For example, walking, jogging, swimming, yoga or tai chi can all be peaceful, but I would not include competitive sports. My personal recommendation is to do the exercise outdoors in nature, but others might say differently. Make sure that your mind is not being stimulated by music, conversation or electronic images, and it is just in a calm, intuitive state, lulled by the rhythm of the exercise. You are now ready to start the visualisation.

Being childish: The behaviour of small children is naturally spontaneous and intuitive. You can access a quietened mind by copying the physical movements of children when they are having fun in the park – for example, stamping in the puddles, kicking the leaves, climbing a tree or blowing bubbles (you're never too old to blow bubbles). You are now ready to start the visualisation.

Before or after sleep: In the 10 or 15 minutes before or after sleep the thinking mind switches off, leaving the brain in a lulled state of semi-sleep. This is another good time to start visualisation.

Because visualisations are done using the non-thinking brain, they can be remarkably powerful but they can disappear with the rapidity of dreams. Try to write them or draw them into your journal as soon as possible. A few sentences are all that is necessary as a memo.

Creative visualisation

Creative or positive visualisation uses the power of the emotions and the imagination to create new and desirable results. Visualisation is used by many sports men and women in the form of mental training and goal setting. They deliberately visualise making repeated, perfect movements for their sport, mentally practising them with awareness of all the senses. Both research and successful field results have shown that this does improve their game. It is sometimes called 'sports visualisation'. The same techniques have been used by patients in hospital to get well, changing their focus from the current discomfort to the delight of walking out of the hospital. It can be used to speed up healing, reduce pain, lower fatigue and increase well-being.

Visualisations like these change the brain patterns, which in turn changes or improves muscle memory. In *The Brain that Changes Itself*, Doidge (2007) writes:

One reason we can change our brains simply by imagining is that, from a neuroscientific point of view, imagining an act and doing it are not as different as they sound. When people close their eyes and visualise a simple object, such as the letter *a*, the primary visual cortex lights up, just as it would if the subjects were actually looking at the letter *a*. Brain scans show that in action and imagination many of the same parts of the brain are activated. That is why visualising can improve performance. (pp.203–4)

Doidge goes on to say that the mind is not immaterial, like a sort of soul that inhabits the material brain. Instead, both mind and brain are powerfully connected. He writes:

We have seen that imagining an act engages the same motor and sensory programs that are involved in doing it… Everything your 'immaterial' mind imagines leaves material traces. Each thought alters the physical state of your brain synapses at a microscopic level. Each time you imagine your fingers across the keys to play the piano, you alter the tendrils in your living brain. (p.213)

This is why sports visualisation is so effective, and why the same techniques can be used for healing the physical body. What is less easy to explain is why positive visualisation can change the outside world as well. Authors writing about the Law of Attraction (Hicks and Hicks 2004; Losier 2007) propose that visualisation techniques can be used to manifest an increase in income, possessions, job prospects, relationships and so on. If you are sceptical about this, think about the odd coincidences that have happened to you already. For example, you think about a friend and suddenly they phone you; you want some information from a book, and it opens within a page or two of what you need; you have entered a full car park just knowing that there will be a space for you, and a car vacates the parking bay in front of you; or you phone up your dentist or hairdresser to find that someone has just cancelled the very appointment that you were hoping to get. These are all examples of the synchronicity that occurs when you have a strong, clear intention. In other words, you engaged with creative visualisation, although it was not done consciously or deliberately.

Creative visualisations are at their most effective if you can get into a cheerful mood while doing them. Try to access feelings of contentment, happiness, exhilaration, bounciness or laughter. One way is to get yourself into a happy mood by remembering other things that have gone well for you. Tap into those memories where you felt excitement, happiness or joy, and, holding on to that cheerfulness, do the visualisation. Another technique is to imagine yourself bubbling over with excitement when your visualisation provides you with what you want – and then use that same feeling while you are doing the visualisation. Gawain (1978) writes in *Creative Visualization*:

> When using affirmations, try as much as possible to create a feeling of belief, an experience that they can be true. Temporarily (at least for a few minutes) suspend your doubts and hesitations, and put your full mental and emotional energy into them. (p.39)

Before you start a creative visualisation, make sure you are absolutely clear about what you want: both in the general feel of the outcome and the specifics. If it helps, make a list of what you don't want in order to clarify what you do want – and then destroy the list of what you don't want.

If you're using words as part of your visualisation (and most people do), make them into strong positive statements and affirmations. Think and write in the present tense, not in the future tense. If you use the future tense, everything will always remain in the future, while using the present tense draws what you want towards you. You also need to put all your statements in the positive form rather than the negative. This is affirming what you do want, not what you don't want. For example, you can say, 'I am financially free,' rather than, 'I am out of debt.' Or you can say, 'My practice is thriving,' rather than, 'I'm through that bad patch.'

Creative visualisation is at its best when it is done with commitment and good intention. You cannot use it to harm other people. Doing a visualisation in this way is an act of creativity, so have fun and enjoy the process of doing it. If you are doing your visualisation in your mind, make a memo of what you have imagined in your journal. If you're working on paper, have fun with the layout. Make it simple but dramatic, using different colours, shapes or lines, drawings or cartoons. Add the details such as how many, what type, where this will happen and by what date you want it to be achieved. Then add some clear, direct affirmations. You can add emotional content either through the colours, or through the affirmations.

Some people like to finish their visualisation with a statement such as, 'All this happens or something better, for the greater good of all concerned.' After you have completed your visualisation, you can relax and let go of it. Close your journal; the job is done. You don't need to review it or repeat it. It is more likely to manifest with one powerful and dedicated session (even five minutes' worth) and letting go, rather than half-hearted frequency.

Letting go is an important step in the visualisation process. It is one of the ironies of visualisation that the more you try to *make* something happen, as if you're demanding something from God or the universe (whatever they mean to you), the less likely it is to happen. If you are striving for a specific outcome, often it is your ego that wants to be in control. If you are demanding an outcome from an energy greater than yourself (God or the universe), it is probably your ego again, which needs to be put aside.

If you feel you need to explain why you want something, you're focusing on not having and feeling the lack — which creates a negative visualisation, providing you with more of what you don't want. Research into the power of prayer has shown that a prayer that focuses on 'Thy will be done' is much more effective than a demanding prayer that says, 'I want'. In the same way, a relaxed or playful attitude to visualisation is far more likely to have results. A gentler way of visualising that still keeps you in both the positive and the present tense is to begin with the phrase, 'Wouldn't it be nice if…?'

Hicks and Hicks (2004) write in *Ask and It Is Given*:

> The reason that the *Wouldn't It Be Nice If…?* game is so important and so powerful is because when you say 'Wouldn't it be nice if…?' you are choosing something that you want but you are being soft and easy about it. In other words, it is not the end of the world. (p.227)

Finally, having let go of both the visualisation and the expectation of results, feel free to follow your intuition and any impulses to take positive action over the next few days or weeks. This might be the universe giving you a nudge. Don't struggle or push to manifest your visualisation, but follow your impulses with a light heart. They might take you where you want to go. They are simply the next logical step.

Some creative visualisation techniques

There are no right or wrong ways of doing creative visualisation and, if you have already found a technique that suits you, continue with it. Here are some suggestions, but feel free to adapt them into something that really works for you.

Daydream your perfect future: Relax your body and mind, and spend some time imagining what you want and filling in the details. If the visualisation is that of designing and creating a new future for yourself, allow your imagination to take you in new directions and embroider each fantasy as you go along. Feel excited by your thoughts and fantasies. Not everyone sees pictures when they imagine things and it is okay to imagine in words. Write a brief memo in your journal of your daydream.

Write a list: Relax your body in one of the ways suggested earlier and, working quickly and intuitively, write down in your journal as many points as you can about the finer details of your visualisation. As you write your list, keep it all in the present tense, as if it is happening now. If you write in the future tense, it will remain in the future, out of reach. Try to write at least 50 points or more, including some playful and fun ideas that make you smile.

Write a screenplay: Quiet your body and mind and have fun writing the screenplay of your life as you'd like it. Write in the present tense and describe how you see yourself spending your days. Include what you are doing, who you are with, where you live and how you get your income. Give it plenty of detail and feel-good ideas.

Make a storyboard: Put all your work and chores to one side and breathe slowly and deeply for five minutes. Collect pictures from magazines and free clipart from the internet to make a visual montage of all the elements you want in your life. Include positive newspaper headlines and a photo of yourself. Make it bright, colourful and cheerful.

Draw your future. Relax into some creativity as you draw what you want to happen. Use colours that feel positive to you and expansive shapes. Write a brief memo in your journal of your drawing and describe how it makes you feel.

Try these exercises for creative visualisation.

Exercise 1

Sit in a quiet place where you will be undisturbed for 10 or 15 minutes and do a short relaxation. Then gently focus on some happy memories to lift your emotional energy. When you feel good, turn your attention to something you want, such as an aspect of your practice or your relationship with a client or colleague. You're going to request this from the universe, so in your mind write it in the air or invent imaginative pictures like a movie. When you have created these wonderful scenarios for your future, enclose your fantasy inside a bubble. Visualise the bubble floating into the sky and into the universe beyond.

Letting it float off into the universe symbolically reminds you that you need to let go of it. Write a few notes in your journal and close the page.

Exercise 2

Think of something that is worrying you; something that you would like to have a positive outcome for, but that you keep turning over in your mind because you have doubts about whether you can achieve it. Examples could be starting up a new clinic, taking on extra patients, returning to being a student after a long absence from study, or moving to a new area and starting afresh.

First of all, write out a clear statement about what you want, phrasing it in the positive and the present tense – for example, 'I am doing the extra work and I find that it is easy, fulfilling and financially rewarding.' As it is quite likely that in doing this you won't fully believe these words, now is the time to remember other things that have gone well and introduce a feel-good factor.

The next step is to have fun and be playful. You do not need to think or work hard, just have fun in a child-like way. Look on the internet for any free clipart that represents your positive outcome, and, using this as a basis, add lots of positive comments. Experiment with using different fonts. You can use the autoshapes on your computer to add smiley faces, sunshine or callouts (the speech or think bubbles that are used in cartoons). Allow yourself to spend time on this, and get immersed in the creativity. When you have finished, save it in your journal folder on the computer or print and paste it into your journal.

Exercise 3

Think of a goal that you have for the future, such as expanding your business, doing more studying or getting a promotion. Then think of a fairy story or favourite movie that will act as a metaphor for your goal, and have fun weaving the goal and the story together. Make notes in your journal.

Here are a couple of different journal examples for creative visualisation.

JOURNAL EXAMPLE

I have got my interview on Monday, and I'm feeling nervous about it. I really want the new job, but it will be a board interview with three people and oh! it feels like walking into the dragon's cave where they might spit fire at me.

My positive statement is: 'I am exactly the person they are looking for, we get on really well in the interview, and I am thrilled that they are offering me the job.' I've been very lucky getting jobs up until now, and for my first job as a teenager I was actually headhunted! I'm going to have fun putting together a visualisation to clarify what I do want (see Figure 8.1).

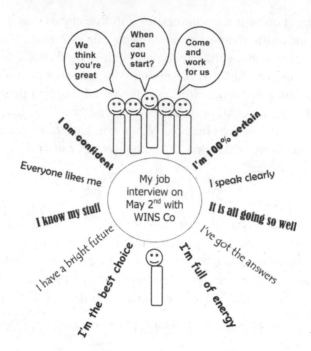

Figure 8.1 Computer-generated creative visualisation for a successful interview

JOURNAL EXAMPLE

I want to increase my practice. I feel ready to take more patients now, so I did a couple of positive visualisations to kick start everything. I started with a short meditation and relaxation session. In the first visualisation, I played with the image of the Sleeping Beauty story. Perhaps my practice was like the Sleeping Beauty, all in perfect order but surrounded by thorny bushes. Someone would have to hack back those bushes to allow the patients to come in.

In the second visualisation, I sat quietly and simply thought about the front door to my clinic – the door through which all my patients will come. In my imagination I cleared all the clutter around it, getting rid of the coats and boots on the inside and cutting the hedge on the outside. I looked the door over carefully and decided that it needed a thorough clean. I made sure the bell worked correctly and I oiled the hinges. I checked whether it would open and close easily and bought a new doormat, one of those with 'Welcome' written on it. I contemplated my front door and felt very pleased with it. Finally, when I was ready, the doorbell rang and I opened the door to find several patients waiting there for me. I greeted them happily.

This visualisation made me feel really good, and a few days later I had an impulse to wash my real door, clean the glass and vacuum the carpet. I have removed the boots as I had done in my visualisation and put some fresh flowers on the little table in the hallway. I feel both my clinic and I are ready for the new patients!

Exploratory visualisation

Exploratory visualisation can be done in order to review a known situation or to explore what is unknown. An example of a review would be to ask yourself how you are feeling about your practice, supervision or business at the moment. Further examples of reviews are to assess how you are getting on with a client or looking at your success or satisfaction levels with your work.

Other uses of exploratory visualisation are to find answers to issues that puzzle you or confuse you. In this case, the visualisation helps to open up your blind spots. Exploring puzzling issues can be done in a left-brained, systematic way, such as those suggested in previous chapters. For example, you might look at your strengths and weaknesses around the issue, or you could look at other people's viewpoints. This could reveal a lot and be very useful, but it takes determination and honesty to do the work thoroughly when you are working on your own. The very nature of blind spots is that they are difficult to identify.

Working with a supervisor or critical friend is an effective way of unravelling puzzles, because they will hold the overview and encourage you to investigate further. Using a visualisation is a completely different way of looking at the issue that takes away the pressure to be systematic but still allows for deeper insights. As Schuck and Wood have said: 'Things that supervisees were avoiding or hesitating to look at directly, reveal themselves through indirect methods' (2011, p.69).

Exploratory visualisation takes you on a symbolic journey that represents an exploration into the unconscious. The thinking brain is deactivated through relaxation, and emotions, words and images are allowed to arise spontaneously. After the visualisation has been completed, and you have come back to the present, you can start analysing what you have seen.

The question that needs to be asked is how reliable these spontaneous words and images are. Could they be wishful thinking, or the invention of a sleepy mind? An intuitive leap can be completely sound or it can be questionable. I suggest that the measure of the accuracy of intuitive understanding is in the resonance felt by the journal writer. If a hidden truth has been unveiled, there is an ah-ha moment of pleasure, relief, surprise or shock. It feels true, and resonates on a deep level. Of course this new understanding can be further investigated using more systematic analysis.

Exploratory visualisation needs to be done with good intention, and should begin with a short relaxation and meditation. Empty your mind of all expectations before you begin, and allow the process to unfold spontaneously. There are no right or wrong ways of doing it, and you can either follow one of the schema set out later or follow your intuition about what will work for you. If surprising or unexpected images come up while you're doing the visualisation, don't attempt to change them, but just accept them and examine them much later after you have completed the session.

I suggest that you don't try to analyse what you have discovered in your visualisation too soon after doing it. It is better to have a break from it, at least for the time it takes to drink a cup of tea. The other advantage of drinking something at this point is that it firmly brings you back to the real world after being in a deep meditative state.

Some exploratory visualisation techniques

The nature of exploratory visualisation is that you are trying to uncover blind spots or information filed in the unconscious. The techniques that I suggest all have the purpose of investigation but go about it gently and softly, lifting the corner of the curtain rather than breaking down the door.

The hero's journey

Because you are seeking understanding or knowledge, one method is to take yourself on a journey in the manner of the mythological hero or heroine. Do a short relaxation of both body and mind. Start your journey in a place of safety, perhaps somewhere you have been to in the past – for example, a beach, a flower garden, a hilltop or beautiful woodlands. You can start in your own home if you prefer. In your imagination, walk from this safe place through a doorway, gateway or portal to a new, different place. Look around this new place for a while, and then walk through a second portal to a place that is unknown, darker or more uncomfortable.

Symbolically, passing through two or three portals or doorways takes you to deeper levels of the unconscious. You can do the same thing by going down staircases or walking downhill in your mind. As you reach your destination, you can find the information you seek being held somewhere sacred, such as in a decorated casket or in a chapel, or it is spoken to you in the words of a wise counsellor or knowledgeable beast.

Lost property

Take some time to relax your body and mind. In your imagination, walk through a small town with shops and cafés to the lost property office. Fill in the appropriate form, and wait while an official goes away and returns with a package. Leaving the office, walk to a quiet park where you can sit and open the package to discover what is inside. As this is your lost property, you will reconnect with something from your past.

Pandora's box

Relax your body and quiet your mind. Take yourself on a journey, from your favourite place, through fields, to a dark wood, to a small cottage, to a small room where you find an intriguing antique box that you cannot resist opening. Four or five positive qualities and four or five negative qualities come out of the box. Without trying to manipulate the results or change them in any way, notice what you have been given. The last thing to come out of the box is hope.

Free drawing

Quiet your mind as you collect up your art materials, and take a few deep breaths. Take a soft pencil and scribble freely across the page using big arm movements. Notice what you can see within the scribbles and take a pen or felt-tip to clarify the images that arise. Colour them in or develop them further if you wish. When you have finished, sit back for a while before trying to make sense of it.

Try these exercises for exploratory visualisation.

Exercise 1

Spend a little time relaxing your body and quieting your mind, following one of the suggestions earlier. Think about the relationship that you have with a line manager, boss, mentor or teacher, either now or in the past. Ask yourself if there is a metaphor that would describe your relationship with them. Sit with this and don't force it. Allow a metaphor in words or an image to come to the surface from your subconscious.

You might want to do a little cartoon sketch of this in your journal, or search for some freely available clipart. Otherwise, write a brief sentence or two. When you feel ready, ponder a little bit on the metaphor you chose, and see if you can learn more from it. Do you need to do anything about this new understanding? Does this lead to an action plan? If this was a past relationship, maybe there is nothing you need to do.

Exercise 2

Take some time relaxing your body and quieting your mind. Remember an occasion where you couldn't make up your mind. However big or however small the issue was, you were finding it very difficult to make a decision.

Take yourself on a guided journey, starting off in a place that is safe and familiar. Go through a doorway or portal, following a clear pathway into an area that is wild and strange. Eventually, you come to a fork in the road and have to decide on which direction to take. You are puzzling about what to do when an animal or bird comes up to you, and tells you that it will be your guide. Notice what sort of animal this is. You ask your animal guide about the two pathways, and it explains to you where each path will lead, and offers to guide you down the path that will be the most beneficial for you. You both follow the path that it has suggested and you feel completely safe in its company. At the end of the path, you're given a special gift, and then the animal or bird guides you back to your starting place.

Give yourself plenty of time to come back to the present, and take a hot drink or some water if you don't feel fully grounded. Then examine what you discovered. What animal or bird was your guide? What did they say about the two pathways? What was the special gift? What can you learn from this?

Exercise 3
Do a written review in your journal of one area of your life, such as your work or your relationships with colleagues at work. Write everything that you consciously know about this, both good and bad. Then do an exploratory visualisation with the specific intention of uncovering some blind spots about the same subject.

Give yourself time to do a short relaxation, and then take yourself on a guided journey, starting off in a safe and familiar place. Pass through one or two different portals, going to more and more unfamiliar places, and arrive at a place where you feel the answers will be revealed to you. The answers can be given in visual, verbal or symbolic form, so don't question anything that arises in your mind but just stay with the visualisation until it feels it has concluded. In your visualisation, you might want to walk back to your starting place, which was safe and familiar, but you don't have to.

JOURNAL EXAMPLE

I am self-employed as a part-time teacher in three different establishments, and I am a visiting lecturer at the university. I have done a written review of all four different jobs:

Venue 1: I've only worked there for a year, and the travelling is terrible!! But all the other teachers are great, and my class is a reasonable size. I like working there because I get a lot of autonomy and can choose most of what I teach.

Venue 2: Student numbers are low throughout the college, and I guess there is the possibility of closure if they don't build up soon. My students have bonded well, even though they are of mixed age range.

Venue 3: My class is a good size, and they are learning well. There is a good atmosphere, and I enjoy teaching them. The old building is a bit grim but they keep it reasonably clean. Staff meetings are unpleasant and can be argumentative.

University: They make the classes as big as possible, because there is a recession on and they need to save money. The students here are the youngest of all the groups, and I have to be very strict about ground rules. But they have accepted me and my ways, and we get on well together.

VISUALISATION TO FIND OUT MORE

I started off in a rose garden, enjoying the beauty and the scent of the roses. There was a hedge around the garden and I had to follow it round to find the garden gate. The handle was stiff, and I went through the gate to find a path through a pleasant woodland with wild flowers. It was much less cultivated than the rose garden, but I enjoyed it very much. I came to a stream and followed it downhill and the landscape became progressively more rugged. I came to a cliff with a fence around it and an old gate. I pushed open the gate and cautiously began my way down the cliff path towards the beach. A thought came to me that I would see my four different teaching venues represented here.

I came to an ancient gun turret, empty since the Second World War, and realised with a shock that there was a man inside who was holding a gun. He was spooky and I walked away as quickly as I could.

I came to a part of the path that was rocky and unstable. I found I was fine as long as I placed my feet very carefully, and then the path evened out and the view was fantastic.

I came on to the beach where a group of young teenagers were running up and down and flirting with each other. I couldn't help smiling as I watched them, and they waved at me.

Another group of older women and children were having a picnic on the beach. They seemed to be having a good time, but the tide was coming in and they would soon get wet. They didn't seem to realise this (see Figure 8.2).

Figure 8.2 Painting representing four aspects of teaching as part of exploratory visualisation

REFLECTIONS AFTER VISUALISATION

I started off in a rose garden and ended up on a beach – symbolically I see both of these as nice and comfortable ('life's a beach'!). The young teenagers who were flirting are clearly the university students, and it was nice that I smiled at them and they waved back. The mixed group of women and children having a picnic close to the tide coming in is probably venue 2, which might close. The difficult journey down the cliff path feels the same as my journey to venue 1.

My biggest surprise is venue 3, which is held in an old Victorian school building and was represented by the ancient gun turret. But the spooky old man with a gun! I have always felt uncomfortable at the staff meetings and this has made me realise how wary I am of the principal. He really isn't a pleasant man, and clearly doesn't like the students. I need to think further about minimising my contact with him, or risking coming into confrontation. Possibly he could fire me. In the visualisation he might have fired at me.

Here is another example of exploratory visualisation.

JOURNAL EXAMPLE

There are times when I get on very well with my boss, and there are other times when I get exasperated with him. I spent a few minutes meditating and then searched around for an image or metaphor that would suit him. Pretty soon it came to me that he is like a bull in a china shop, while I am the china shop retailer. He's a friendly bull, he's not angry, he's not pawing the ground, and he's not going to charge. But with every movement he makes he is bound to crash into something, and I'm watching with bated breath. How he ever got into the china shop, I don't know (see Figure 8.3).

As I did the drawing of him, I wanted him to be a bull with a big smiley face that wants to make friends with everyone. I wonder how many people just see 'bull' and feel frightened, and how many people see the smiley face and the twinkle in his eyes? He is a kind man and very well intentioned, but he lacks basic social skills. He tramples over people's feelings without noticing.

I didn't put me into the drawing but I'm standing on the sidelines watching this happen. Sometimes I can gently direct the bull, and sometimes I can protect the china, but sometimes I just have to witness the breakages. He upsets people, tramples on their feelings, takes them for granted, and is considerably surprised when they leave.

Figure 8.3 Drawing of a bull in a china shop, as part of an exploratory visualisation

It becomes clear to me that I'm not going to change this bull at all. He's never going to become a soft-footed cat in the china shop. Whoever put him there made a mistake, but he's in there now and he will continue hurting china despite his good intentions. What I can change is my own reaction to it. If I continue to get exasperated, or continue to wait with bated breath to see what will happen next, I will only damage myself. I must get myself into a more neutral place, and to do this I will visualise that I'm standing behind a glass screen (reinforced, bull-proof), watching at one remove. What will happen will happen. I cannot protect everyone he comes into contact with, and I cannot blame him for his big feet and clumsy nature.

Maintenance visualisation

It is difficult to feel peaceful and cheerful when the mind is full of anxiety, negative thinking or limiting beliefs. Sometimes it feels really good to do a version of space clearing for the mind, getting rid of unwanted clutter. In this section, I give suggestions about letting go of anxieties and persistent thoughts.

When you are in the grip of negative thoughts, they can dominate the mind. Here are some examples, where the mind gets stuck in the past, present or future. Some people dwell on conversations they have had in the past and, while their mind replays the exact words or actions of their antagonist, they are inventing a better script for themselves. Other people might be like the needle stuck in the vinyl record, continuously bemoaning the discomfort of their present situation, such as their relationship, their job, their income or their health. Still others might be thinking ahead to a future situation where they will have to deal with more than usual, such as a presentation at work, a necessary confrontation or travelling to a new destination. Their minds invent a whole range of different problematic or unpleasant scenarios, adding to the feelings of stress.

Another form of negative thinking comes up when there are limiting beliefs. These often come from a misinterpretation of parental messages, leading to a life script that limits them in some way – for example, people who say, 'I'm the stupid one in our family' or 'I've never been any good with computers or technology.' Limiting beliefs can also come through copying family traditions of limiting potential, such as 'Our family are not fond of exercise' or 'I wouldn't trust the food if I went abroad. My dad was like that as well.'

Another problem that comes up for some people is when they start worrying about or trying to control the other people in their lives. Byron Katie (2002), writing in *Loving What Is*, describes how we get caught up worrying about other people's stuff, when there is nothing we can do about it:

> I can find only three kinds of business in the universe: mine, yours, and God's. (For me, the word *God* means 'reality'. Reality is God, because it rules. Anything that is out of my control, your control, and everyone else's control – I call that God's business.) (p.3)

She goes on to say:

> If you understand the three kinds of business enough to stay in your own business, it could free your life in a way you can't even imagine. The next time you're feeling stress or discomfort, ask yourself whose business you're in mentally, and you may burst out laughing! (p.3)

There are many different ways of emptying your mind of negative thoughts and unnecessary anxiety. The aim of all of them is to quiet your mind, reduce stress and create space for forgiveness, either of yourself or of others. As with the other forms of visualisation, you should start with clear intention of what you want to achieve, and work using the non-thinking brain, accessing intuition and spontaneity.

After completing your maintenance visualisation, it is good to do a ritual cleansing of yourself. This can be done in the physical real world or just in your imagination. You can have a complete shower, or just thoroughly wash your hands, or close your eyes and imagine yourself doing these. You can mime washing your hands, rubbing them together without the soap and water. You can do an energy cleanse without getting undressed, vigorously brushing your body all over with your hands, starting at the top of your head and sweeping down your torso, your arms and legs.

It is quite surprising the way the universe will provide the answers if you take the time to do space clearing of your mind. You will wake up the next morning with an answer to a question, or you will open a newspaper at random and find the information you need is in front of you. People with whom you want to talk will spontaneously phone you first, and the bus will arrive just as you walk up to the bus stop. I remember a time when I was quite worried about a discontented cat that was living with us. I handed the problem over to the universe and promptly forgot about it, but within a week I was browsing through a charity shop looking for something else when I came across an excellent book on cat management.

Some maintenance visualisation techniques

The aim of the maintenance visualisation is to reduce anxiety and increase calmness and self-esteem. Some people like to include a longer portion of meditation to achieve this. There are no right or wrong techniques. Do whatever works for you.

Reprogramme the child that was you

This can take 15 or 20 minutes. Sit quietly and do a slow, gentle meditation, listening to your breathing and relaxing both body and mind. When you feel ready, imagine that you are in a really safe place, in a building or outside in nature. Become aware of this place, and notice its colours, sounds, smells, tastes or touch. Slowly walk around the safe place until you come to a doorway, gateway or entrance. At the entrance there is the small child that was you, aged five, six or seven. Give your child self a hug and tell them that you love them. Then very gently tell them:

- they are a wonderful person

- they are beautiful/handsome and clever

- they deserve everything in this life

- the world is their oyster

- they deserve money, success, health, happiness and anything else that you know you would appreciate.

Hug your child self again and let them take you by the hand to meet with yourself as a teenager or young adult. Give this self a big hug, and slowly, gently tell them the same things.

Finish with telling your child self and young adult self that you love them very much, and wave goodbye to them as they leave the safe place. Gently come back to the present. Make some notes in your journal.

Make a mind map

Take a few minutes to relax your body and mind. Draw a mind map or spidergram in your journal, showing all your tasks and all your anxieties about those tasks. The advantage of a mind map is that it can show the interconnections between everything, mimicking the busy wiring of your brain. When you have completed this, clarify which are your business, which are other people's business, and which belong to God or the universe (whatever these mean to you). Be honest with yourself about this. If you're worrying about someone else, or criticising them, or concerned about their opinions, you are in their business. If you're worried about natural disasters, or problems of the nation, or war, you are in God's business. These are things you cannot change, however much you worry about them.

After you have finished, identify any issues that are definitely your business and draw a big circle around them or use a highlighter pen. Notice how few issues you are left with, compared with the original mind map. These are the truly important issues that will benefit you to take action on. Finish with doing one of the cleansing rituals.

Make a list of what you want

If you have a vague discontented feeling or a free-floating desire for something better, it can be difficult to identify the precise nature of what you want. Begin with a few minutes of relaxation and meditation. Then write a list of what you don't want on a piece of scrap paper. This will help you clarify what it is you do want, which will go on a new piece of paper or into your journal. The wanted list might prove to be the polar opposite of the unwanted list, or it could trigger new ideas. Once you are satisfied that you have chosen a really good list of what you want, have fun destroying the unwanted list. Cross everything out, scribble over them, screw the paper up into a tight ball, burn it, tear it up or destroy it in any other way. You could fold the list into a little paper boat and drop it into a stream to float away. It would be good to use washable ink for this one, so that the worries wash away. A character in Charles Dickens' novel, *David Copperfield*, writes all his worries on to a kite and flies them as far away from himself as possible. Finish with one of the cleansing rituals.

Pack up your old kit bag

Close your eyes and take a few minutes to listen to your breathing and relax all the little muscles in your face. Then visualise writing each worry on to a separate piece of paper. Each piece of paper is then carefully folded, packed neatly into tissue paper and placed in a strong wooden or metal box. These boxes are all placed in a suitcase, which feels very heavy when you pick it up. You carry the heavy suitcase (with difficulty) to the junk room, attic, basement or garage in your house and put it where it can be kept for long-term storage. You can even post it abroad to the polar ice cap or the darkest jungle. Feel the relief of having got rid of it and not having to carry it any more!

By the time you get round to reopening all the boxes, you won't even be able to remember the nature of your anxieties. Finish with one of the cleansing rituals.

Use borrowed sentences

Borrowed sentences come from other people's conversations or fragments of written work. You can utilise these as triggers for reflection or visualisation. For example, a hoarding poster might tell you, 'life is better with…' or a newspaper headline says, 'Wins £10,000'. You don't need to read any further; just take the phrase and play with it, providing your own suggestions to complete the sentence. Another example is that someone passes you by on the street, talking to their colleagues or into their phone, and you overhear a single sentence that has meaning for you. Treat all these as advice from the universe and take some quiet time to think about their relevance. Finish with one of the cleansing rituals.

Ask the universe to do it for you

Breathe deeply for a few minutes, consciously relaxing all the little muscles of your face. Ask God or the universe to deal with a large proportion of your concerns or tasks. It is best to do this in writing, dividing the page into one-third for your responsibilities and two-thirds that you will give to God to deal with. It can be a relief to 'let go and let God', but you cannot hedge your bets by continuing to worry: you have to let go completely and trust in your visualisation. Finish with one of the cleansing rituals.

Try out one of these exercises for maintenance visualisation.

Exercise 1

Think of an unresolved issue in your life, a question that tugs at your brain and might even disturb your sleep. Sit with your eyes closed or looking at something neutral. Relax your body and quiet your thinking mind using one of the techniques described earlier. Visualise that you are walking up a steep hill in the countryside, with a packet of colourful balloons in your pocket. When you reach the top of the hill, it is a beautiful, fresh summer's morning, with blue skies and a brisk wind chasing clouds across the sky. Taking out your balloons, blow up several of them and, using a big felt-tip pen, write your issue on to the balloons, one word on each balloon. Choose the colours of the balloons carefully and have fun writing one word on each. Then stand up with all the balloons in your arms and let them fly out into the wind, jumbling up your sentence and carrying your worries out into the sky. Enjoy the moment! Then finish with one of the cleansing rituals.

Exercise 2

Review all your relationships with family, friends and colleagues. Choose someone who irritates you. Start with writing a list of all their faults as you perceive them. Even if your inner voice tells you you're being unfair or prejudiced, write everything down until you have vented them all out of your mind. Then ask yourself if it is true, and gently laugh at yourself for your exaggeration. Destroy the list by scribbling over it, tearing it up, burning it or anything else.

Now write a new list in your journal. Begin this list with the other person's positive qualities, whether big or small. For example, they have a nice smile, they sent you a Christmas card last year, they get on well with other people, they are tidy or their emails are always to the point. Try to put between five and ten items on this list. Then in your role as fairy godmother or benevolent sorcerer, give them the beautiful gift of another five or ten positive qualities. Pick out qualities that will benefit them, such as happiness or a loving relationship. You know that if they are happy all their relationships will improve, including the one with you. Finish with one of the cleansing rituals.

Exercise 3

Take a new page in your journal and draw a line down it dividing it into one-third and two-thirds. In the smaller portion, write the heading, 'Things I will do today', and in the larger portion write, 'Things I want the universe to do'. Start with your personal list, writing down the things that you will realistically achieve and you really intend to do. Then consign everything else to the universe, and trust that doors will open, opportunities will arise and things will work out for you. Try to be very clear about what you want the universe to do, writing short, positive sentences in the present tense. Remember to focus on what you do want, not what you don't want. Have good intention towards other people so that your visualisation benefits them as well.

After you have written your two lists, read them through and say gently to yourself something like:

> Wouldn't it be nice if all these came about. I love the idea of such a simple life, just handing everything over to the universe. I will do my allocated tasks for today, and I will let go of everything I have written on the universe's list. I trust it will be provided.

JOURNAL EXAMPLE

I'm really busy at work, getting ready for the presentation in two days – there is still so much research to do – and I've got to set up my projector slides – and my suit needs to go to the dry cleaners – and I was going to work late tonight and then my brother phoned up and said could I join him for a drink as it's his birthday – and I haven't got him a present – and I need at least six more illustrations for my projector slides – and there's a meeting tomorrow morning – and tomorrow night I can't work late either...

I think it's time to hand some of this over to the universe (see Figure 8.4).

What I plan to do today and tomorrow	What I want the universe to do
Do one hour extra work this evening and then meet my brother	Enable me to work quickly and efficiently all day tomorrow
Buy something for him on the way to the station	Provide me with time and space to work, with the minimum of interruptions
Focus on my research all tomorrow	Give me the absolute minimum of phone calls
	Enable me to be very fast and efficient with any phone calls that do come
Go for a walk in my lunch break to get some exercise and fresh air	Allow me to have a refreshing lunch break taking my walk in the sunshine
	Inspire me about where to research for the presentation
Take suit to cleaners at the same time	Enable me to distil the ideas into brief presentation slides
	Find me some good pictures to put into the presentation
	Provide a card or present for my brother

Figure 8.4 Asking the universe to do it for you, as part of maintenance visualisation

REFLECTIONS THE FOLLOWING WEEK

The presentation went really well, and I don't know why I got into such a twist about it. It was really very straightforward. My brother had loads of suggestions for illustrations (I bought a bottle for his birthday by the way) and as luck would have it my boss had to cancel the morning meeting, which gave me extra time. And a weird thing happened: my phone got turned off accidentally, so I had a silent morning in which to work!

CHAPTER 9

REFLECTIVE WORKSHEETS

In her hands
the bunch of yellow daisies
brightens her smile

A worksheet is traditionally a printed sheet of paper with questions that a writer is expected to answer directly on the page. There are many interesting worksheets and questionnaires available that inspire self-reflection. Their basic function is to help writers understand themselves and to uncover blind spots. They give structure and direction to the self-reflection, and in this respect they are very similar to reflective cycles (see Chapter 7).

At the most basic, some questionnaires are written for fun, such as those published in popular magazines. These questionnaires might be focused on the reader's lifestyle, attitude to work, relationships or understanding their psychological type. Having completed the questionnaire, readers can then work through the scorecard to find out if they are type A, B, C or D. Each type is described and differentiated from the others. These questionnaires are great fun, but they do not produce any great insights.

There are a lot of more serious psychological questionnaires available. These can present from six questions up to dozens, encouraging the writer to reveal their psychological profile. Most of these questionnaires have a list of positive statements with multiple choice answers graded from 'strongly agree' to 'strongly disagree'. The results of the questionnaire are calculated through a scorecard system. Good examples of these can be found on the internet, such as those on psychological well-being, satisfaction with life, subjective happiness, gratitude or self-esteem.

These sorts of questionnaires have two functions. They can be used as survey material for someone collecting data, and they can be used by the person doing the questionnaire as a tool for self-understanding. They are relatively quick to do, and some of the questions can produce interesting insights, even before the results are calculated, simply because they have never been thought about in that way. I have recommended these questionnaires to students working on their personal development plans. If one of their strategies is to improve well-being in some way, such as taking up regular exercise or meditation, doing a questionnaire is an excellent way of measuring well-being before and after engaging with the strategy (see SMART objectives in Chapter 7).

My focus in this chapter is on a different type of worksheet that contains a minimum of questions and necessitates that the writer thinks deeply and writes considered answers. Of all the various types of worksheets and questionnaires, these contribute the most towards self-development, because they force people to find their own individual answers. There is no scorecard at the end but significant learning about the self. These worksheets can be used once as an investigation, or they can be used again and again as different issues arise, even on a daily basis. If they are repeated, they become a record of change and development.

Each worksheet begins with the negative emotional stance currently being experienced by the journal writer and helps them to make changes, often by investigating the thoughts and beliefs behind the emotions. Another way of saying this is that each worksheet begins with the voice of the inner Child that is emotional and unreasonable, then starts to work with the calm, rational inner Adult or occasionally the mature, comforting inner Parent.

Transformation using worksheets

There are so many overlaps between a reflective framework and a worksheet that I could have put them together in the same chapter. To differentiate them, perhaps we can say a reflective cycle is more likely to begin with a specific incident, while a worksheet is more likely to begin with an emotional feeling or reaction, although this is not a hard and fast rule. The reflective cycle is often work orientated, helping you identify troubling incidents, analyse them, understand them and move forward. The worksheets I am presenting here focus on your feelings, encouraging you to shed limiting beliefs and become more positive for greater health and peace of mind.

It is human nature to feel a whole range of different emotions, and they are all natural and appropriate when they arise spontaneously in an appropriate situation – for example, grief after a bereavement or fear in front of a wolf. They are at their most healthy when the negative emotions such as fear, grief or anger are expressed honestly and openly and then allowed to pass away. If they can be fully accepted and experienced in the moment, they will disperse. Problems arise when emotions are expressed inappropriately and too often, such as fear when there is no wolf – or not expressed at all, and therefore suppressed.

The emotions have a profound impact on health levels and, as an alternative health practitioner for over 20 years. I have met numerous examples of this. One woman told me how she created a severe headache simply by being really angry and raging at her children. Another young woman lost her voice with acute laryngitis when she was indignant but could not express it.

Children display the link between their emotions and their health levels very clearly – for example, the child who feels they are not getting enough love, perhaps because the mother has gone back to work, or there is a new baby, or the mother herself is ill. These children can develop chronic colds, coughs, sticky eyes and ear infections, as well as dermatitis and eczema. Frequently I have observed this type of child to be immature, clingy and have separation anxiety. Treating the children holistically brings the emotions back into balance, making them less clingy and more independent, and it frequently clears up the physical symptoms as well.

It is my observation that negative emotions disrupt health, while positive emotions enhance it. If you take the time to work with your emotions, using self-reflection or worksheets, you can make big improvements in your health and well-being. Lipton (2005) writes in *The Biology of Belief* about his experiments as a cell biologist and his discoveries concerning how all the cells in the body are affected by the thoughts:

You can live a life of fear or live a life of love. You have the choice! But I can tell you that if you choose to see the world full of love, your body will respond by growing in health. If you choose to believe that you live in a dark world full of fear, your body's health will be compromised as you physiologically close yourself down in a protection response. (p.113)

Beneath the emotions, and often directing them, are recurring patterns of thought and a structure of beliefs that hold people back from flourishing. Belief structures can be very strong and create very clear boundaries, utilising words such as 'ought', 'can't' or 'shouldn't' – for example, limiting beliefs about being unable to be successful, earn sufficient money or even to enjoy your work. These beliefs might have been inherited or originally created as a protective device, but in the long term they are limiting. They create many fears, low self-esteem, lack of energy and eventually poor health.

Examples of limiting beliefs are easy to find. Compare the businessman who feels overworked and develops chronic disease with his counterpart who is stimulated by his work and thrives on it. Compare the pregnant woman who believes she will have a difficult childbirth and becomes so tense that she needs a lot of intervention with her counterpart who is confident in her ability to have a natural childbirth and has an easy experience. Look at the war veterans who have been told that they will live a limited life of disability but their determination and strong belief in themselves have enabled them to become top athletes. Lipton says: 'When the mind changes, it absolutely affects your biology' (2005, p.111).

As well as having a deep influence on your health and well-being, limiting beliefs can hold you back from progressing in many areas of your life, such as in education, careers or relationships. A lot of beliefs are set up before the age of seven, and they can be very deeply rooted even though they have no solid, logical foundation. A belief that originates in your early years often has other members of the family subscribing to it, which appears to give it verification. When your beliefs are challenged, it can lead to discomfort and resistance. Even when a negative belief is outdated and no longer useful, it can be rigidly held on to because of its familiarity. Here is Lipton (2005) again:

Your beliefs act like filters on the camera, changing how you see the world. And your biology adapts to those beliefs. When we truly recognise that our beliefs are that powerful, we hold the key to freedom. While we cannot readily change the codes of our genetic blueprints, we can change our minds. (pp.112–13)

It is only through conscientious work on yourself that limiting beliefs can be cast aside, opening up limitless possibilities for the future. Negative thought patterns that have gone on for years can be dispelled and replaced by an easygoing cheerfulness. I would like to differentiate between actively changing your beliefs and the habit of talking positively as a mask over patterns of inner negative beliefs and emotions. The latter is sometimes called 'positive thinking' but it is a superficial top layer that does not make any changes to the inner beliefs. It is looking on the bright side without believing in the brightness. It can actually increase suffering because of the disparity between reality and hope.

The real work of changing your inner beliefs and emotions is often slow, depending upon your (often unconscious) resistance, but once done it is profound. This is more than positive talking – it is a complete change of attitude. Changing inner beliefs can be done with the help of a therapist, a supervisor or a critical friend, all of whom can take the role of an impartial observer. Limiting beliefs can also be shifted through writing in your journal, especially when it is honestly self-reflective and challenges the self. But if you don't have a methodology, it can be tough going, especially if you have many blind spots.

Worksheets are an effective way of stripping away negative beliefs and their emotions, by defeating them through logic or by deliberately climbing up the cliff face from negativity into positivity. They can be used on a day-to-day basis, removing each short bout of negativity as it occurs and gradually reframing the whole attitude. This is transformation indeed, leaving only a sense of well-being, cheerful positivity and maybe spiritual comfort as well.

Worksheets demand that you take full responsibility for your life and interactions with other people. However provoking other people are, it is each individual's choice how they react to them. This can feel like a difficult burden to carry at first, because it is much easier to blame someone else, but eventually it becomes liberating to know that you are in charge of your own thoughts and feelings, and nobody else is.

Hicks and Hicks (2004), writing in *Ask and It Is Given* takes the work out of worksheets by calling them processes or games, and encouraging the writer to have fun at the same time:

> We use the words *process, technique,* or *game* interchangeably because, while these are powerful processes that will assist you in achieving anything that you desire, if you will take a playful approach to them, you will hold far less resistance than if you see them as tools to fix something that is broken. *The key to the success that you will find in these processes actually hinges upon your ability to release resistance, and the more playful you are, the less resistance you hold.* (p.139; emphasis in original)

In the rest of this chapter there are various worksheets, and I suggest that you try them in their original form at first. After this, you can research others or design your own worksheet if you find a format that provides you with more insights.

Moving up the emotional scale

Much as we would like to, it is almost impossible to jump from really negative emotions such as fear, grief, depression, guilt or rage to happiness, joy and zest for life. The emotions won't allow it, and trying to think positive thoughts when you are in a negative mood feels hollow and insincere. Moreover, if you try to force yourself into being positive when you are really low, you will start to feel out of alignment with your true self.

What you can do, however, is to improve your emotions bit by bit, like climbing up a ladder. If you imagine that all your emotions could be graded between extreme depression and extreme joy, each small step up from the bottom is a definite bonus, providing a measure of relief. Here is a tentative scale of emotions:

1. Joy/Knowledge/Empowerment/Freedom/Love/ Appreciation

2. Passion

3. Enthusiasm/Eagerness/Happiness

4. Positive Expectation/Belief

5. Optimism

6. Hopefulness

7. Contentment

8. Boredom

9. Pessimism

10. Frustration/Irritation/Impatience

11. Overwhelment

12. Disappointment

13. Doubt

14. Worry

15. Blame

16. Discouragement

17. Anger

18. Revenge

19. Hatred/Rage

20. Jealousy

21. Insecurity/Guilt/Unworthiness

22. Fear/Grief/Depression/Despair/Powerlessness.

I have taken this list from Hicks and Hicks who qualify it, saying: 'Since the same words are often used to mean different things, and different words are often used to mean the same things, these word labels for your emotions are not absolutely accurate for everyone who feels the emotion' (2004, p.115).

Your task is to use this scale, or another like it, consciously to climb up the ladder of your emotions. An example would be that, if something happens to make you feel depressed, changing your thoughts to feel anger is an improvement. Some people might think that anger is equally destructive, but compared with depression anger is a lot more proactive and flexible. Another example would be if you feel frustration or irritation at something but manage to shift your emotions up to boredom. Boredom takes you away from the minutiae of the frustration, and gives you a glimpse of the bigger picture, helping you to feel better. A further example is doubt, which leaves you standing on very unstable ground, unable to know what to believe. If you manage to move your emotions up to disappointment, the ground is much steadier; you can recognise what to believe although you feel sad that it has not come up to your expectations.

The first step is to acknowledge your current emotions, accepting them without criticising yourself. They are not wrong. They are what they are. Give yourself some quiet time, and then see if you can move up the emotional scale. Sometimes you will be able to take yourself step-by-step all the way up from a negative emotion to a positive one. At other times you will only shift one or two steps. But the overall effect is cumulative so that each time you are less likely to drop into the negative emotions, and when you do it is easier to come out of them. Here are Hicks and Hicks (2004) again:

> There is tremendous value when you are able to *deliberately* cause even the slightest improvement in the way you feel, for even in that small emotional improvement, you may have regained a measure of control. And even though you may not have fully exercised your control to bring yourself entirely back into the full connection with your full power, you no longer feel powerless. And so, your trek back up the emotional scale is now not only possible, but it is relatively easy. (p.117, emphasis in original)

Exercise 1
Bring to mind the person who most irritates you at work, either the heart-sink patient or the colleague that you don't get on with. Write about them very briefly in your journal, and identify where you are on the emotional scale when you think about them. Search around to find some aspect of working with them that makes you feel better, and write this down.

Continue this process of consciously reaching for the best feeling thought you can find, and start to move up the emotional scale. Continue as far as you can go.

Exercise 2

Do a mental scan of your moods over the past few days, and identify one instance where you felt quite low down on the emotional scale. Write briefly in your journal about what happened and identify your key feeling at the time. Then search around to find some aspect of the incident that makes you feel better and write it down. This might be something very small, but it must resonate with you as emotionally better for you. In consciously acknowledging that the new emotion feels better than the previous one, you have begun to move up the emotional scale.

Sit with the new feelings for a few minutes, then search around to find another aspect of the incident that makes you feel better still. Continue up the scale as far as you can go, feeling each emotion fully and acknowledging its truth for you.

JOURNAL EXAMPLE

A new patient came for her first appointment on a Saturday last month. I have been a shiatsu practitioner for a year, working on Wednesdays and Saturdays with my day job for the rest of the week. My new patient seemed a very pleasant woman, dressed in expensive clothes and driving a powerful car. We arranged for her to come back after two weeks for the next appointment, but she didn't turn up and didn't answer my phone messages. I still had to pay my clinic rental fees. Later in the week she phoned to apologise, saying she had only just realised she had missed the session. Apparently she hadn't got my messages. She booked in for the next Saturday.

Again she didn't turn up and again I had to pay clinic fees for a room that I didn't need. I sent her an invoice for two missed appointments, but she emailed me to say that both times it had been a genuine mistake and she didn't think she needed to pay.

- I felt *powerless* when she refused to pay.

- I have no way of reclaiming the clinic fees and the time wasted on a Saturday afternoon.

- I hate this sort of *helplessness*; my hands are tied.

- I am *angry* with this patient for messing me around.

- I feel *indignant* that she has no consideration and thinks she can just not turn up.

- I still have to pay the clinic fees: I can't tell the manager it was a genuine mistake.

- I am *angry* with myself because I should have questioned why she didn't receive my phone messages after the first missed appointment.

- I am *discouraged* because I thought she had read my terms and conditions flyer.

- I am *worried* that I might get more patients like that.

- I *blame* myself for believing her after the first missed appointment and booking her in again.

- I am *disappointed* because she seemed a nice woman – and she seemed to be wealthy.

- I am *impatient* to get more genuine patients.

- I don't have the time for time-wasters.

- I want to forget about this woman; I'm *bored* writing about her.

- It's water under the bridge. I've learned from the experience.

- I would like to visualise more genuine patients.

- Perhaps I will offer a three-appointment package if they pay upfront.

- I'm feeling more *optimistic* now.

- I don't have to let this bother me any more.

- I am *optimistic* that I will get loads of nice patients from now on.

- I will do my visualisation.

- I am eager to meet my new patients!

Finding the feel-good factor

When something goes wrong it is human nature to want to think about it and analyse it. The problem is when it becomes a temporary obsession, taking over a large amount of your waking thoughts for a day or two. The mind can become quite hyperactive on the topic, reviewing what actually happened, rewriting history, planning retaliation or rehearsing improvements. All this achieves is to keep you in the same unhappy, uncomfortable place. What you really want, what you are yearning for, is the polarity position of things going really well for you. This is the reason for the obsessive thinking.

This worksheet can take 15 or 20 minutes of quite intensive thinking but the results are rewarding. You begin with deciding on two statements. The first statement describes the situation as it is now, focusing on your negative feelings. The second statement takes you into the polarity position where you feel so positive and cheerful that life goes very smoothly for you. Don't expect other people to change: just see yourself with a different attitude. Place these two statements on the page with a large gap between them. It doesn't matter if you want to work from the top of the page to the bottom, or start at the bottom.

Now the real work begins, as you search for thoughts that you can write in the space to help you bridge the gap between the two statements. These thoughts must be positive and make you feel good, but at the same time they must be congruent for you. It's no good writing that you would feel better if you were immensely rich or powerful, because this is probably not going to happen in the next few weeks, and you would feel the discord between this wish and reality.

Here are some suggestions about what you can write, but don't be limited by my list. You can use anything that makes you feel good. Try to find at least ten feel-good thoughts that will help you smoothly bridge the gap between your two statements.

- Remember a past time when things went well in a similar situation.

- Remind yourself that things go well for other people.

- Move away from the specifics and generalise – for example, 'Most of my life is good.'

- Remember some small thing that lit up your day, such as the sun shining or someone's smile.

- Remind yourself of any strategies you might have, such as visualisation.

- Remind yourself of the unconditional love that you get from your pets.

- Remember the last time you laughed.

- Choose a cheerful metaphor to reframe how things are going for you at the moment.

- Remind yourself of the people you love.

- Remind yourself of the things you love in and around your home.

- Design a possible action plan.

Exercise 1

Practise reframing negative statements into positive ones. Choose a negative thought about a client, about your practice, about your personal appearance and about your home. With each of them, write out a negative statement, and then write out a positive one. The statements can be two or three sentences. Do not generalise, but give each statement in the first person, using 'I' – for example, 'I am embarrassed and humiliated by the fact that my eyesight has deteriorated and I'll have to wear glasses. I feel I look awful in glasses.' The positive statement could be, 'When I look back through my photos I can see how many times my appearance has changed over the years. I accept that wearing glasses is another change that I will get used to very soon. It will be wonderful to read easily!'

Exercise 2

Begin with writing a statement in your journal about something that has happened that makes you feel unhappy or irritable. Be brief and to the point, and take full ownership, writing, 'I feel...' For example, 'I feel really fed up when I hear my mother's complaining voice on my messaging service.' Then, leaving a large gap on the page, write the polarity statement. This needs to have the feel-good factor, and feel congruent for you. Staying with the same example, I could say, 'I feel happy and cheerful and I am blessed to have a good relationship with my mother most of the time.'

Try to find at least ten feel-good thoughts that you can write in your journal to bridge the gap between the two statements.

JOURNAL EXAMPLE

I feel I don't have time to do any exercise. I have three small kids and I work part-time as a Reiki practitioner, so I'm always rushing around. I would love to feel better about myself, but I'm so exhausted at the end of the day that all I do is collapse in front of the TV.

- When I was a teenager I used to feel great after exercise.

- When I was living in Bristol, I used to walk to work and think nothing of it.

- Other people allow themselves the time to go to an exercise class or to the gym.

- People say that they feel healthier and have more energy when they do regular exercise.

- I would be a better role model for both my kids and my patients if I did regular exercise myself.

- I could start with one hour a week at the gym. That's not too much.

- I could walk up the stairs at work instead of taking the elevator.

- I could take the kids to the park more often. They could go on their bicycles or scooters and I would have to run to keep up with them. That way we would all get exercise!

- I could give myself Reiki or go to my colleague once a week in the evening for Reiki. That would boost my energy much more than watching TV.

- I would have more self-respect if I knew I was taking better care of my body.

- It is springtime, and the days are getting longer, so it is an ideal time to start.

I feel really happy and healthy now that I am doing regular exercise. I know that I deserve the time for myself, and everyone benefits because I have more energy.

Four key questions

The following method has been taken from Byron Katie (2002) in her book *Loving What Is*. It is a worksheet that examines your attitudes towards other people, and in doing so reveals your underlying beliefs and self-judgements. It is deceptively simple, using just four questions that go to the heart of the matter. In using it, you will loosen fixed beliefs that you have been tied to for many years, and you'll come to a much more peaceful state of mind.

This worksheet is based on the premise that all suffering comes from believing our thoughts. When you believe your stressful thoughts you feel miserable, but when you deeply question them you will feel liberated from them and peaceful. This method, which is known as 'The Work', has been used around the world for everything from racial prejudice to cancer.

You begin the worksheet with writing about someone else from an emotional standpoint. You make short sentences about how they irritate you, how you want them to change, what you think they should or shouldn't be doing, what you need from them, what you think of them, and what you don't want to experience again with them. Katie (2002) calls this the Judge-Your-Neighbor Worksheet. She writes:

I invite you to be judgemental, harsh, childish, and petty. Write with the spontaneity of a child who is sad, angry, confused, or frightened. Don't try to be wise, spiritual or kind. This is the time to be totally honest and uncensored about how you feel. (pp.11–12)

Then ask the four questions that start you on a process of insightful inquiry. The first two questions are to check the truth of your original, emotional description. You will probably find that you have no evidence for the truth of your statements. They might feel emotionally true to you, but actually they are untested theories or stories of the type that everyone invents to make sense of their world. The second two questions examine the impact that your thoughts have had on you, and what life would be like without the thoughts. Let the answers to these four questions arise spontaneously from within, if you can.

The final part of this worksheet is called the 'turnaround'. This is the process of inverting or swapping over the characters or the emotions in your story. You experiment to see what it would feel like taking the other side. For example, if your original statement was, 'I get irritated when my partner doesn't appreciate me,' you could turn this around to, 'My partner gets irritated when I don't appreciate her.' See what this feels like and what you can learn from it. Then you can try another turnaround, such as, 'I get irritated when I don't appreciate her' or 'I get irritated when I don't appreciate me.' Sometimes you can take the negative position, and look at, 'I don't get irritated when my partner doesn't appreciate me,' or 'I don't get irritated when my partner appreciates me.' When writing these turnarounds, you ask yourself whether any of them is closer to the truth than the original statement.

Katie says, 'The turnarounds are *your* prescription for healing, peace, and happiness. Can you give yourself the medicine that you have been prescribing for others?' (2002, p.16, emphasis in original).

Exercise 1
Next time you hear a voice in your head, saying that you or someone else 'should' do something, make a note in your journal. Apply the four questions to it. Is it true? Can you

absolutely know that it's true? How do you react when you think that thought? Who would you be without the thought? Write some notes about your discoveries in your journal.

Exercise 2

Write in your journal a prejudiced assessment of another person. Allow this to be an outpouring and write plenty, but write it in short statement-like sentences. Write about how they irritate you, how you want them to change, what you think they should or shouldn't be doing, what you need from them, what you think of them, and what you don't want to experience ever again with them. When you have finished, ask yourself the four key questions with reference to what you have written, taking it sentence by sentence. Allow the answers to drift up naturally to the surface of your mind.

1. Is it true?

2. Can you absolutely know that it's true?

3. How do you react when you think that thought?

4. Who would you be without the thought?

Finally, work with the turnarounds and, taking each of your original sentences in turn, experiment with exchanging your own position with that of your antagonist. See what this feels like and whether it feels true for you.

JOURNAL EXAMPLE

WHO ANGERS OR SADDENS OR DISAPPOINTS YOU?

I am angry with Brian at work because he asks for my suggestions but never takes my advice. I am angry because he is egotistical and arrogant. I am irritated that he talks louder than everyone else. I hate it when he interrupts me with his own ideas.

HOW DO YOU WANT THEM TO CHANGE?

I want Brian to listen to me when I make suggestions. I want him to tone down his loud voice. I want him to learn from other people. I want him to do his paperwork more often. I want him to wash up his own coffee cup.

WHAT IS IT THEY SHOULD OR SHOULDN'T DO, BE, THINK OR FEEL?

Brian should be more considerate. He shouldn't ignore me. He should keep his desk more tidy. He should spend less time with personal phone calls.

DO YOU NEED ANYTHING FROM THEM?

I need Brian to work as a team with me. We're supposed to be a team. I need him to treat me as an equal, because we are on the same pay level.

WHAT DO YOU THINK OF THEM?

Brian is selfish. Brian is egotistical. He only thinks about himself. He is messy.

WHAT IS IT YOU DON'T EVER WANT TO EXPERIENCE AGAIN WITH THAT PERSON?

I don't want to work with Brian if he continues to be so selfish. I don't ever want to work in such an unequal team again.

INVESTIGATION OF THE FIRST SENTENCE

I am angry with Brian at work because he asks for my suggestions but never takes my advice.

1. *Is it true?* No, it's not true because occasionally he has taken my advice.

2. *Can you absolutely know that it's true?* No, I can't know it's true. Maybe he has taken my advice more often than I have realised. Sometimes he thinks very fast and takes my suggestions one step further.

3. *How do you react when you think that thought?* I feel fed up and indignant when I think that he is ignoring me. I feel foolish when I think he never takes my advice.

4. *Who would you be without the thought?* I would enjoy working with Brian because he is lively and quick thinking.

TURNAROUND ON FIRST SENTENCE

I am angry with Brian at work because he asks for my suggestions but never takes my advice.

- I am angry with myself because I'm full of suggestions but I never take my own advice.

- Brian is angry with me because he asks for my suggestions but I never give any advice.

- I am angry with myself because Brian has lots of suggestions and I never take his advice.

- Brian is angry with himself because he asks for my suggestions and doesn't take my advice.

- I am angry with Brian because he never asks for my suggestions, and cannot take my advice.

WHICH ONE OF THESE IS TRUE FOR ME?

- It's true that I am bad at taking my own advice.

- It's true that sometimes I have turned down Brian's advice.

- It's true that I would be angry with Brian if he never asked for my suggestions.

Cup half full

In some situations it is easier to turn away from the negative emotions, in a short, sharp swap to the opposite perspective. This is the difference between seeing your cup half full instead of half empty. The issue does not change, but your attitude changes so it no longer irritates. You are not just talking positively, but spending time to find the genuine advantages of the same situation. This in turn invites more desirable experiences into your life, whereas the negative thoughts simply invite more negativity (see positive visualisation, Chapter 8). Here are Hicks and Hicks (2004) again:

> We encourage you, very strongly, not to beat up on yourself when you recognise that you are feeling negative emotion. But as soon as you can, stop and say, *I'm feeling some negative emotion, which means that I'm in the process of attracting what I don't want. What is it that I do want?* (p.254; emphasis in original)

It is very helpful to use the emotions as a guidance system. If there is something that you are persistently thinking about that makes you feel miserable, it is probably time to look at the positive aspects. This might feel difficult at first, until you remind yourself that nobody can know the full story about anything. Everyone constructs a version of the truth out of what they perceive, but there are always blind spots. Looking at your cup half full will produce a story that is just as likely to be correct as the previous one, but it has the advantage of feeling more comfortable and more positive (see narratives, Chapter 3).

This worksheet has two sections: the current negative viewpoint with the cup half empty and the new perspective of the cup half full, where there is compassion towards the self and others. You can have fun turning the page around and writing the changed perspective from the opposite direction.

Exercise 1

Think of a holiday that you had where something went wrong – for example, the plane was delayed, your car ran out of petrol, you forgot to bring something, or you didn't like the food at the hotel. Write down in your journal your negative feelings about this holiday and allow yourself to be as childish and unreasonable as you like. Make it clear that this is your negative list by decorating it with dark colours, lightning bolts or frowning faces.

Write another list about the same holiday, taking the opposite point of view, and highlighting the positive things, such as 'We met some really interesting people' or 'The wonderful market added a sense of adventure to the day.' Don't rewrite history or invent what didn't happen: just cherry pick the better moments. Include some compassionate comments about the other people on your holiday, such as 'The waiter was charming and hard-working and didn't deserve the bad temper from the other people' or 'The bus driver remained calm despite all the traffic.' Add some bright colours, sunshine motifs or smiley faces.

In doing this exercise you are making a deliberate decision about whether this holiday will go down in history as the holiday where everything went wrong, or as another pleasant holiday that you enjoyed.

Exercise 2

Bad news always seems to sell better than good news, so there is a constant flood of shocking, sad or negative news on the internet, TV, radio and in the newspapers. Try taking an item of recent news and turn it around to the positive. For example, focus on the family who survived, rather than on their house that was damaged by the gas explosion; or focus on the good work the politician has done, rather than the scandal about his driving.

Reflect on the impact of all this negative news, and whether it would change much if it was presented from the positive. What would the effect be on your mood, your outlook on life, or on society?

Exercise 3

Using your journal, write about a client, patient or colleague who is causing trouble for you at the moment – for example, upsetting you, irritating you or not coming up to your expectations in any other way. First of all, write about the situation as you perceive it, including your emotional reactions, even if they are irrational. Then change your perception to view the same situation from a completely different angle.

JOURNAL EXAMPLE

THE PROBLEM AND MY INITIAL THOUGHTS

The receptionist at the clinic is lazy and inefficient. We are a multidisciplinary clinic and it is her job to talk to new clients and give them an outline of the different therapies so that they can choose the one that will suit them. But as far as I can see she hasn't bothered to read the flyers, and she only has a very hazy idea about some of the therapies. Mostly she directs people towards massage or beauty therapy, or she looks at the diary to see which therapist has got an appointment available. As she is a single-parent mum, she has to have a phone on all the time in case the nursery phones up. It seems that a lot of her friends phone up as well.

I'm really concerned about her behaviour because it has a big impact on my practice. I need more clients!

I have asked the other practitioners how they feel about her. The massage and beauty therapists are pleased with her work – well, they would be, wouldn't they? But the shiatsu practitioner, the acupuncturist and I (the reflexologist) feel that we are missing out and not getting enough clients. I asked the practice manager to do something and she said she would, but she doesn't like confrontation and never got around to it. Finally, I tried to have a word with the receptionist when everything was quiet and asked if she fully understood about the different therapies and whether she wanted me to explain anything, so that she would be able to tell prospective clients. She gave me a funny look and said she understood all of them.

I have come to a deadlock. I don't seem to be able to make any changes to the situation, and I'm getting very negative about it. I'll see if I can change my point of view.

MY CUP IS HALF FULL

I enjoy working in a multidisciplinary practice. There is a cheerful camaraderie among the different practitioners and therapists that makes it a pleasure to come here. It was opened originally as a beauty clinic, and there has always been a slight emphasis on beauty therapy and massage. The advantage is that the therapy rooms look very attractive with polished wooden floors and fresh colours. We are very lucky that we have the front door on the high street (although we are upstairs) and this gives us a prominent presence and inquiries from passers-by.

The stairs from the front door lead up to the reception area, which is rather cramped and the only room that doesn't have a window. I feel sorry for the receptionist working there because it is not such a nice atmosphere. However, she is a cheerful woman and always has a nice smile and a pleasant word for clients who are in the waiting area. They feel comfortable and relaxed with her. She enjoys chatting with the therapists when they have their lunch break, and generally likes to laugh. If she's got nothing to do, she phones a friend.

She seems to give out more appointments to massage and beauty therapy than the alternatives, but maybe that reflects the people who live in this town. I understand that it is not her job to help me build up my practice. That is my responsibility. In future I will make sure there are enough flyers for passers-by to pick up. I will ask the manageress if the alternative therapists could make small, tasteful posters to put up in the reception area, or the corridor – or even in the bathroom! I will see if I can write a small advertising feature for the local paper.

REFLECTIONS

I hadn't realised I was being so negative! I was blaming the receptionist for everything, turning her into the scapegoat for all my problems. No wonder the practice manager forgot to have a word with her. She was very wise not to collude with my assumptions about the receptionist. It's time I took more responsibility and stopped casting myself as Victim, with the receptionist as Persecutor – and then expecting the manageress to Rescue me.

CHAPTER 10

REFLECTING ON REFLECTION

Peaceful evening
the beauty of sunset
formed by clouds

In Chapter 2, I made a few recommendations for working with the reflective journal. It's useful to return to these after three or six months to reflect on whether you've been following them, and, if not, why not?

Choose an attractive format: Are you satisfied with your choice of journal, whether computer, paper or sketchbook? Some people are comfortable writing in any format while others are more sensitive and need to work with materials that resonate with them. Make sure that you have the tools that suit you, so that it feels good to sit down and reflect in your journal.

Use it often: Have you managed to include regular reflection into your schedule? Some people like routine and others prefer to be spontaneous. Either way, try to use the journal often, and allow yourself to write brief notes if you don't have much time. The more often you can open the journal and write something, the easier and more familiar the process will be.

Work with freedom: Are you giving yourself permission to work in any style or method? Many people find they have been so strongly imprinted by their school experiences that it feels quite difficult to break away from a formal writing style. But if you allow your inner Child the freedom to play and experiment, you can have fun at the same time as learning about yourself.

Dare to go: Can you ask yourself tough reflective questions? At first it can feel very unsettling to question your beliefs and attitudes, especially if you have had these for a long time. Self-questioning and replying with honesty can be your biggest challenge. But after a while it can feel liberating. You will emerge from the constraint of outdated beliefs, negative thinking and narrow horizons – and develop into the empowered adult that you want to be.

Watch out for your inner judge: Are you being too hard on yourself? Your inner judge is like the critical Parent, always ready to find fault with you and minimise your successes. When asked to weigh up strengths and weaknesses, the judge only notices what you did wrong. To counterbalance it, you can evoke your inner free Child, and allow yourself to feel pleased with success, however small it is. Imagine a small child jumping up and down and clapping their hands. Allow yourself to write about what you did well and regularly congratulate yourself.

Watch out for your inner justifier: Are you trying to protect yourself too much? Your inner justifier is like the adapted Child and always wants you to be in the right. The justifier finds it too painful to find fault with you, and resists change. When asked to weigh up strengths and weaknesses, it will notice other people's weaknesses but not your own. To counterbalance it, connect with your inner nurturing Parent, and remind yourself that you're not being blamed for weakness: you're being given the opportunity to develop and improve.

Keep what you write or create: Do you feel the impulse to edit or remove some of your earlier reflections? It might be interesting to view the self-reflective journal as a graph. There will be a lot of individual ups and downs from day to day, but the overall curve demonstrates continued self-development. In this context, it's worth keeping everything. Massive insights can be forgotten if the subject matter goes out of context, and minimal entries that appear to be lacking in depth may contain seeds that germinate later.

Date every entry: Do you remember to date each entry in your journal? You will find it most useful when you are rereading your journal. With hindsight you will be able to make connections that you couldn't see at the time.

Have fun: Have you been able to have fun with your journal? There are all sorts of ways to lighten up. You can get messy and play with your paints and felt-tip pens. You can include things that make you laugh and lift your spirits. You can cut and paste from emails, from freely available clipart, or anything else. You can headline each entry with a smiling face or frowning face.

Be kind to yourself: Can you accept your own vulnerability and need for self-care? Being kind to yourself does not mean releasing the self-justifier but rather using the journal as a place to nurture yourself. If you are a practitioner or therapist, you will be spending many hours helping others. The journal is where you help yourself, nourishing, supporting, investigating, challenging and learning. In this simple act of self-indulgence, you will be helping others after all.

REFERENCES

Adams, K. (1990) *Journal to the Self: Twenty-Two Paths to Personal Growth*. New York: Grand Central Publishing.

Bender, S. (2001) *Keeping a Journal You Love*. Cincinnati, OH: Walking Stick Press.

Borton, T. (1970) *Reach, Teach and Touch*. London: McGraw Hill.

Doidge, N. (2007) *The Brain that Changes Itself*. London: Penguin Books.

Gawain, S. (1978) *Creative Visualization: Use the Power of Your Imagination to Create What You Want in Your Life*. San Rafael, CA: New World Library.

Gibbs, G. (1988) *Learning by Doing: A Guide to Teaching and Learning Methods*. Oxford: Further Education Unit, Oxford Polytechnic.

Hicks, E. and Hicks, J. (2004) *Ask and It Is Given: Learning to Manifest the Law of Attraction*. London: Hay House.

Johns, C. (2009) *Becoming a Reflective Practitioner*. Chichester: Wiley-Blackwell.

Karpman, S. (1968) 'Fairy tales and script drama analysis.' *Transactional Analysis Bulletin 7*, 26, 39–43.

Katie, B. with Mitchell, S. (2002) *Loving What Is: Four Questions that Can Change Your Life*. London: Rider.

Knowles, M. (1973) *The Adult Learner: A Neglected Species*. Houston, TX: Gulf Publishing Company.

Lipton, B.H. (2005) *The Biology of Belief: Unleashing the Power of Consciousness, Matter and Miracles*. Carlsbad, CA: Hay House.

Losier, M.J. (2007) *Law of Attraction: Getting More of What You Want and Less of What You Don't*. London: Hodder and Stoughton.

Luft, J. (1984) *Group Processes: An Introduction to Group Dynamics*. Palo Alto, CA: Mayfield Publishing Company. (Original work published 1963.)

Minton, D. (1997) *Teaching Skills in Further and Adult Education*. London: City & Guilds/Thompson.

Moon, J.A. (2006) *Learning Journals: A Handbook for Reflective Practice and Professional Development*. London and New York: Routledge.

Rainer, T. (1978) *The New Diary: How to Use a Journal for Self Guidance and Expanded Creativity*. Los Angeles, CA: Jeremy P. Tarcher.

Schuck, C. and Wood, J. (2011) *Inspiring Creative Supervision*. London: Jessica Kingsley Publishers.

The Society of Homeopaths (2010) *Code of Ethics and Practice*. Available at www.homeopathy-soh.org/attachments/CodeofEthics_April10.pdf, accessed on 24 September 2012.

Taylor, B.J. (2000) *Reflective Practice. A Guide for Nurses and Midwives*. Buckingham: Open University Press.

Zigmond, D. (2010) *Physician Heal Thyself: The Paradox of the Wounded Healer*. Available at www.marco-learningsystems.com/pages/david-zigmond/physician-heal-thyself-3.htm, accessed on 21 May 2012.

INDEX